AF596795

It's All about Mindset

OUR PURPOSE, JOURNEY
AND SUCCESSFUL LIFE

NILESH POTDAR

INDIA · SINGAPORE · MALAYSIA

Old No. 38, New No. 6
McNichols Road, Chetpet
Chennai - 600 031

First Published by Notion Press 2019

ISBN 978-1-64249-196-8

Cover Page Photograph by Nilesh Potdar.

HC : 9798895190609

To my beloved son Aryan, for giving me the reason to write, to my wife Soniya for her support during the book writing process, to my parents for being there with me always and to my grandmother for being the inspiration to write this book

CONTENTS

PREFACE

What makes us happy and fulfilled? Money, Power, Freedom, Rewards? These things make us happy momentarily, but they don't bring eternal fulfilment in life. Moreover, we start relying on these material things to see ourselves successful and there begins a never-ending quest for gaining more and more to maintain our status quo. These are illusions of the so-called successful life we continuously strive for.

It is an infinite race with life, the race to an unknown destination with a constant fear and vacuum deep within our minds. A race with time. A race full of regret over the past and anxiety about the future. If you win, life loses. If life wins, you lose. It is a lose-lose game, silently leaving behind empty spaces in our minds, and making our lives miserable.

True happiness in life comes from feelings of satisfaction and contentment in every moment of life, irrespective of material possessions. It is a mental state where you are totally independent and free from the race with life.

This book is an attempt to help you quit the dormant state of life and embark on a new success journey. It is full of insights on how to achieve true independence, protect yourself from illusions of success, fine-tune your habits and rituals, invest your time wisely, and be a true human.

We are all a part of the same universe and our purpose in life is predefined by a supreme power. We have been assigned a certain role to achieve set objectives within the given timeframe of our journey through life. Therefore, it is important to understand our ultimate purpose and align all our actions with it.

True joy comes from our connection with the supreme purpose. The universe in itself is a continuous creation process. Our planet earth, biosphere, ecosystems, human evolution, everything is a part of this process. The sustainability of the universe depends on this process. However, as we are busy racing with life, we often get into the illusion that our own happiness and sustainability comes from collecting material things.

We direct all our focus towards securing and collecting and think less and less about creating and contributing. Today, I urge you to protect yourself from this illusion which is keeping you from reaching the ultimate goal of your life.

This book takes you through simple techniques and practical ways to tune in your mindset to the creation and contribution mode. It talks about simple things from day to day life to help you relate to and absorb the thought process presented here. The tools provided in this book are useful for people who wish to take their life to a new level of happiness.

This book helps you get unstuck and shift from a stagnant phase to a creative, happy and fulfilled phase of life. I congratulate you on selecting this book and welcome you to this exciting journey to a new life.

IT'S ALL ABOUT MINDSET

All power is within you.
You can do anything and everything.

– Swami Vivekananda

Let's start our journey with the story of a King, the wealthiest king of all time. His possessions were the largest ever witnessed by anyone in the whole world. Being a King, he enjoyed the prosperity and power of wealth. But with all this power, he was still empty and unfulfilled deep within his mind. The heaps of gold coins, diamonds, pearls and the acres of land could not give him the inner contentment that he relentlessly sought. He could never talk about his internal struggle to anyone around him and felt lonely in the midst of all his riches.

One day, after a music session in his palace, he asked the singer, "What motivates you to sing with such a profound connection with your soul? You don't possess great wealth. You don't possess great power. Then what makes you so content and happy in what you do?"

A pristine smile appeared on the bright face of the singer. He replied in his poetic manner,

"Oh, great King, the supreme power of God enters my voice and makes me sing. Oh, great King, with the spiritual forces of music, I do forget my existence and I do forget everything.

Oh, great King, not from the claps and not from the gold coins you bring, my happiness is purely an internal thing."

The King was stunned by his reply. Something struck his mind as he went into deep thoughts. He felt defeated initially, but he was curious to know the answers he was seeking. The singer further explained, looking at the thoughtful face of the King, "I find happiness from my work, I feel satisfied by my practice routine, I feel fulfilled when people say my singing helps them to connect with their inner peace, I feel motivated when I see there is more to learn every time I practice. No other thing in this world, including wealth and power, can offer me so much contentment in life."

The King could not relate much to his life, but was partly convinced by the words of the singer. With increased curiosity, he asked, "But I am not a singer or an artist; I don't practice like you do. Not everyone can have skills that you have. You are happy just because you are special and gifted with this talent."

The singer started laughing. But as he saw disappointment surfacing, he immediately added, "Oh my great King, as I said earlier, happiness is an internal thing. Every human being is gifted with a powerful mind which has unlimited capabilities. One needs to recognise and appreciate the hidden power of the mind and leverage it to achieve happiness in life.

The mind is so flexible that you can train it the way you want. The world is full of both negative and positive things and one has to be careful in choosing and adopting the right mindset to ensure their own happiness in life."

The King requested him for more insights on the human mind and on how to set the right mindset. The singer continued to explain, "The human mind is one of the most amazing things in the universe with the infinite power of imagination and creativity. We are all gifted with this superpower which enables us to think, analyse, express, communicate and create.

Ever since we entered this beautiful life, all our actions have been driven by the forces of our minds. As we grow, there is a continuous process of training in our minds based on every experience that life brings in. We learn from these experiences and decide our ways of dealing with things and situations. These ways shape our personality and self-image. We chose what is most relevant and comfortable for us and try to avoid all that is irrelevant. These internal developments set our mindset and drive all our choices, actions and reactions. The way we think, the way we look, the way we behave and every single thing we do is driven by our mindset.

The good news is that with the power of creativity it possesses, the mind can transform itself into a whole new state. With the power of training and retraining, the mind has the unique ability to revolutionise itself. We witness great artworks, unbelievable abilities and creations which are beyond our imaginations. They are not lucky, they are not gifted with the right circumstances and they did not have different choices than we did.

They are all humans like you and I, living on the same planet, breathing the same air, drinking the same water and having similar abilities as you and I have. So, my great King, please do not ever think that you cannot be happy. You can be happy in any situation if you have the right mindset. Remember, it's all about mindset!"

As the conversation continued, the singer shared his knowledge and wisdom about setting the right mindset. The King was mesmerised by this new life-changing experience. The singer took him through the complete journey of human life, touching upon the various stages from childhood to old age. The King was astonished to know about the various facets of his mindset, from understanding the supreme purpose of life, being truly independent, empowering the internal forces, using time wisely, connecting with our work, managing habits, taking care of our health, maintaining rituals, and dealing with procrastination and fear.

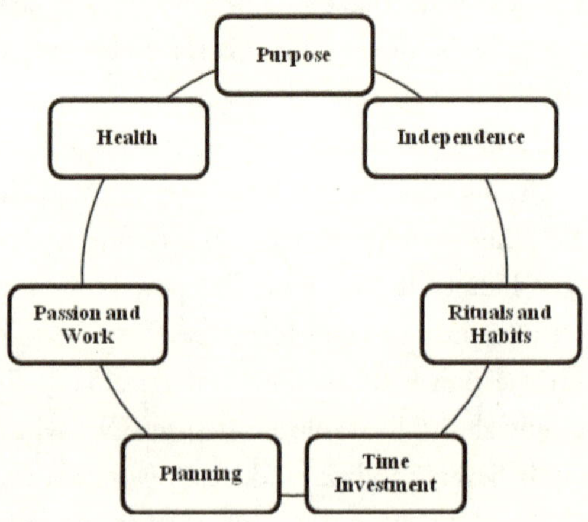

Don't you think most of us are like this King, who is missing fulfilment in his life although he enjoys material success? Some sort of emptiness exists deep within our minds. Even after achieving success in life, we still feel this emptiness. Why is it so? Why is our happiness not certain? What is the reason that even after collecting sufficient material possessions, we are still not complete? What could be the reason that we feel disconnected from our purpose and do not enjoy our work? Why do we get demotivated and knocked down even by small obstacles on our way? How do dependencies and negative habits drag us down?

The answers to these questions will arrive in front of you as you travel through this book. You will find how having the right mindset can help achieve lasting happiness and fulfilment in life. Various techniques are provided throughout this book to help you maintain and protect the happy state of mind irrespective of the circumstances you are in. So, let's begin!

THE SUPREME PURPOSE OF LIFE

I slept and dreamt that life was joy. I awoke and saw that life was service. I acted and behold, service was joy.

– Rabindranath Tagore

One fine day, when Ryan was on his way back home from work, something terrible happened to him. A group of five people with covered faces kidnapped Ryan from a place close to his house. Ryan, before realising what was happening to him, fell unconscious. They took him to a remote place, completely unknown to the 35-year-old Ryan.

After a few hours, when he opened his eyes and tried to shout, the tape on his mouth did not allow him to do so. Someone removed the tape and Ryan kept screaming and shouting for a while. A person with a knife came near him and threatened to kill him if he did not stop shouting. Ryan had no choice but to keep quiet. The man told Ryan that they knew everything about him – his salary, his family, his job and his friends. They demanded a certain amount of cash to release him without any harm. A quick calculation in mind told him that all his savings together come up to this amount. It was evident that they knew every detail of his life. Ryan was now scared. He thought of his wife, his two kids, his parents at home and was worried these people would go to any extent for want of money.

Ryan requested and pleaded for release, saying he did not have that much money in his savings account and that it was impossible for him to arrange the cash. Without listening to any more explanations, two men started beating Ryan. His broken nose and mouth bled, and Ryan fell unconsciousness again, as his head hit the wall. After a while, they woke him up with a splash of chilled water to his face. Ryan was now extremely scared of these people as they were very aggressive.

In the meantime, another group of people entered the room with a hostage. Ryan realised that he was trapped. But what Ryan saw after that was the most horrible and cruel thing he had ever witnessed.

As the hostage refused to agree with the demand of this gang, they shot him dead on the spot. Ryan was now in complete shock. *What if they kill me? What if they trouble my family? What if they keep me trapped for a long time?* Anything was possible. As they turned to Ryan, he immediately agreed to pay them what they wanted. Ryan had to arrange the money by contacting one of his friends. Ryan was finally released after the payment was made.

Ryan is still under shock and thanking God that he is alive. As he reflects on life, he goes through a chain of thoughts. "Life is so uncertain and insecure. Anything can happen anytime, no matter what precautions you take. Why is it so? Is there any way to get certainty in life? Kidnapping, accidents, killing, sabotage, robbery, betrayal, cheating. These things are so common in today's world as if they are a part of life. There is so much negativity all around us. Is it even worth being a nice person? Is it even beneficial to care for others and help others without expecting anything in return? Is life just a competition for survival?

There is no point in praying to God for a good life. At the end of the day, some thief is going to steal everything that you earned honestly by working hard all day. I lost all my savings overnight. I don't know how many more months it will take to rebuild my bank accounts and my wealth."

Ryan went far with these thoughts, beyond his usual limits of imagination. It was the most thoughtful night ever. He was desperate to find answers to all his logical questions. He started thinking about his entire journey in life, right from his childhood memories. "Where did I come from? What is my path? Where am I going? What is the objective? What is the purpose of all this?" His thoughts suddenly paused for a moment. This was the question which struck his mind like lightning. *What is the purpose of my life?* This was the biggest question for him and he now desperately needed the answer without moving any further in this journey of life.

Ryan was still lying on the terrace, observing stars, completely united with his thoughts in a quest to find about his purpose in life. On the one hand, he felt good about his release from the kidnappers, and on another, he was scared about life being highly uncertain. But now one thing was clear to him – it is a waste of life if one does not know the purpose of existence.

"I want to know the ultimate purpose of my life, I want to know the ultimate purpose of my life," Ryan whispered. "Yes. My dear, I have an answer to your question," an unknown voice answered. Ryan looked around curiously, but there was no one. As the voice started to explain further, Ryan quietly kept on listening, as he was more interested in the answer than in knowing the origin of the voice.

"My dear friend, I can understand your dilemma and all

the questions which are troubling your mind at this moment. I am going to answer all your questions in a simplest possible way, so that you can understand it quickly and also share it with others when someone comes to you with similar questions in the future."

Ryan was now listening with great attention. "Listen carefully! I am going to share the bigger perspective of life so it becomes easy to understand our purpose. To begin with this, let us start from our planet. Earth is the only known planet in our galaxy which supports life. Humans are the only living species on this planet that can analyse and understand the concepts of this universe. In fact, humans are created by God to protect this planet which cannot sustain without the creative powers of the human mind.

Animals live with their own limited instinct of survival and do not possess the power to think and analyse. Humans possess the power of thinking, analysing and creating, through which we have changed this planet since the beginning of our existence.

We have separated ourselves from animals and formed our own society. We are spread across the planet and are able to connect and communicate with each other anytime we want. We have created a means of travel that enable us to reach any part of the planet whenever we want. We understand what is good for our planet and make various efforts to save it. We plant trees, we avoid pollution, adopt several measures to benefit nature. We know the importance of natural resources such as water, air and soil and we have created systems to protect these resources available to us. We have even gathered the knowledge of earth's position in our galaxy and have also physically reached some of the other planets in galaxy. Although there are still things unknown to us, we pretty much understand our solar system and the various planets and their characteristics." Ryan was now a bit confused as none one of this was closer to the answer to his questions, but he decided not to interrupt the voice so soon.

"It is not a coincidence or an accident that humans have all these abilities. It is the creation of God with very specific purpose. Whatever features and characteristics we possess are carefully defined and crafted by him. Every one of us is sent to earth with a certain role to perform using the tools that are provided to us. As a part of our definition, we cannot choose our parents, our country and our city of birth, our siblings, colour, appearance, language and so many other basic things. It is all predefined by the creator based on his definition and expectations. But once he sends us to earth, we slowly start understanding life and over time, we develop the ability to choose our path and actions. We go through the journey of life to realise our special gifts, our interests, our inclinations and our inner callings. We get complete freedom to choose our surroundings, people, language, profession, food, habits, rituals we follow and to design our life as we want. With all this freedom available to us, the success of our life depends on two important aspects. First, 'How we fulfil the purpose of our life' and second 'How we experience the journey of life'

Now, it is very important to understand the fact that the purpose of life is set by the creator and is left to us to understand while the experience of life is our choice.

Our motivation and hope come from actions which are in line with the purpose of life and also give us inner fulfilment, whereas our enthusiasm and our energy levels come from our experiences in the journey of life. The success of human life largely depends on how we achieve these two aspects through various phases of our life, from childhood to old age."

Ryan was now extremely eager to know the various phases of our lives, our purposes in each of these phases and how to ensure that we fulfil our purpose and get the best experience out of this life. He felt as if a tremendous energy was travelling through his body and refreshing him. He was getting close to the highest knowledge of his life, the fundamental things which need to be understood by anyone who wants to live a meaningful life with happiness, fulfilment and true independence. As the voice unlocked these insights, Ryan kept listening to it inquisitively.

"God has designed our life cycle with four important phases: childhood, teenage, young age and old age. Each of these phases has a specific importance and purpose and the success of every phase contributes to the overall success of life. Let me talk about each of these phases and its purpose.

Childhood is the first phase of the human life cycle. It starts at birth and ends when we start developing our understanding of the world, as we enter our teenage years. Childhood is like free-flowing water which occupies any space available to it and adapts to any colour which is added to it. It is truly unconditional and knows no boundaries or restrictions for itself. It is wide open to receive everything exposed to it, including the good and the bad. The purpose of this phase is to enjoy the gifts of life and experience the abundance of love, joy, randomness and freedom.

Being the most innocent and purest phase of our entire life, it is the primary phase where our life gets shaped and forms the foundation supporting the further journey of life. The values we learn and life as we get to know in our childhood becomes our permanent impressions about life. Our experience of childhood sets the tune for the next phases and determines how we approach our life in future. Without enjoying childhood, a human cannot understand the importance and abundance of true joy that life offers.

The second phase of life is when we reach adolescence. As a teenager, we still have all the freedom that we had in our childhood, but in addition, we now understand ourselves more. We can think and have opinions about things, choose our interests, follow the successful people and trends and set our paths and directions as we go through this phase. The main purpose of the teenage years is education, knowledge and self-development. This is an important phase to start developing the skills required for life, for professional development, for health and for the mindset.

This is the phase where we plan our life's journey and find our potentials and interests. This is the phase where we understand the requirements of life, choose the right track and the right people as friends and mentors who can guide us and expedite our progress, choose the right books to read and gather knowledge from and meet the right group of people to get more exposure to various aspects of life.

Teenage is the phase with maximum energy when compared to all other phases of life and it is the best time to develop physical strength, vitality and a healthy lifestyle. Teenage is the phase where you develop a strong foundation of health, knowledge and mental strength, which helps us in our next phase of life when we actually need to use all of these tools in our day to day life.

The third phase of life is the young age or mid-age when we start our professional and family life. This is a very crucial phase of life where most of us face rough waters through which we have to navigate. The purpose of this phase is to plan our finances, build our career, grow our families, take care of old people who are dependent on us and also guide the youngsters around us when they seek our mentoring.

This is a phase where you have to plan for your future requirements of wealth, health and happiness. This is the phase where you have maximum responsibilities and roles to play in your life such as a parent, mentor, guide, teacher, motivator and so on. This is the phase where your contribution to the world actually starts. As you go through this phase, you are expected to motivate and direct the new and upcoming generation, and help them set the right goals and find their purpose in life.

You are also expected to help the aged people who need physical and mental support to keep themselves happy in the remaining span of their life. The interesting thing here is that as you mentor the teenager, you are using the experience of your previous phase to help them. And as you support the old age people, you understand their problems and the limitations that life brings with time, which helps you plan your own old age properly, as you can foresee issues from the experience of others.

Without fail, you need to plan your finances required for future expenses, considering your limitations to earn in your old age. In this phase, you also need to spend time on developing your hobbies and interests, other than your profession. It may be a social cause, helping someone, reading, writing, or any other hobby that you love. This time is your investment for the future, when you'll find this hobby as a friend and can spend your time happily on it.

The fourth phase of life is old age, where you have physical limitations and cannot really work like you could in your young age. The age is not the scale and you can choose when to start this phase. For some people, it begins at 60, for others at 70 or 80. It all depends on situations, capacities, the type of work you do and requirements at that point in time.

The main purpose of the old age phase is to mentor and guide the younger generation. All your experiences, your mistakes, your wins, your achievements and your decisions can be invaluable insights for the younger generation, who are about to begin their journey into the initial phases of life. The purpose of this phase is to support the people in all other phases by sharing your experience and helping them make better decisions.

You are an experienced sailor who knows what exactly needs to be done when the sea gets rough and scary, what it takes to achieve great success in life and what the purpose of life is. You, as an accomplished person, are supposed to help next generation to find their own purpose in life. At the same time, this age gets difficult with health and mindset issues. You need to practice gratitude, feel grateful for the journey of life so far, and be happy and fulfilled all the time."

It was midnight by now and Ryan was listening carefully to the insights shared by the unknown voice, which were truly inspiring and motivating for him. However, he was not totally convinced yet. He understood the various phases of life and its purpose as explained by the voice but what about planet earth and the supreme purpose which is defined by God for us. How does the purpose of these individual phases of life help planet earth?

While Ryan was busy thinking about his questions, the voice continued to explain further, "Now, since you have understood the four phases of life and its purposes, it is time to understand how these phases are designed to achieve the supreme purpose of human life on this planet earth. You must have seen how a plant grows from a tiny seed to a giant tree with branches and deep roots. There are phases in a plant's life and every phase has its own purpose. Finally, the plant becomes capable of producing fruits, supporting other lives and creating a strong support for itself. Humans are living systems with the purpose of supporting earth to get better and better every day.

The planet can sustain only with the help of creative species like us; and the most important thing to maintain sustainability is Human Evolution. As humans grow in their abilities, they can strengthen the earth. The whole principle of sustainability is based on the concept of continuous creation and improvements. If we carefully fulfil the purpose of every phase of our life, we can expedite the effectiveness of the process of human evolution. We can minimise the rate of degradation of natural resources, which is essential for the sustenance of the planet's natural systems. We can focus our attention on helping each other to achieve the overall goal of protecting and nurturing this planet.

In today's world of too much distraction and uncertainty, it seems like we are all operating in starvation mode. We all are afraid to lose the game of life. We are too busy collecting material possessions. We define our success by approvals, claps and salutes received from others for our collection. We want more and more of these possessions to see ourselves successful in life. We are trying to run away from uncertainty and in the process, we are getting into a business of grabbing. We have stopped thinking and caring about society as a complete system. Instead, we are in competition with all the other members of this society.

Every day, there is a new standard and benchmark for success, which has to be achieved and broken by some other person to set the new record and so on and on. It's a never-ending race. It's a race against the normal pace of life where the rule is to kill others and survive, instead of collaborating and supporting each other to live together.

Ryan was partly convinced, but then he thought it is very natural. When there are so many of us, there will definitely be a competition to get the most of it. There is nothing wrong with it and, in fact, if we don't compete, we are out of the game and will get killed for our inaction.

The voice continued, "It is important to achieve our milestones in life, meet our financial goals, career and family goals, have a decent lifestyle and enjoy life to its fullest, but not at the cost of the planet. We cannot sell this planet, get money and go to another planet for a new life. What will happen if we collect all the money available on this earth and kill everyone else? Will it be called a victory? Will you be the richest person on earth by doing this? Will you become happy this way? The sustainability of our planet goes hand in hand with human evolution. The earth supports our life and we support its life. This is the basic requirement for ensuring certainty of human life.

Success by collecting is our biggest illusion. You come in life without any possession and in the end, when you leave this world, you cannot take anything with you. You have to leave everything behind. Then what are you fighting for? What are you collecting for? What are you struggling for? I am not saying you should stop earning and stop all your work. My point here is that you should try to understand the difference between financial requirement and financial madness.

You don't need anything beyond your financial security, your own survival, your ability to support your family, ensure their basic requirements and have some provision for times of crisis. Beyond this, I don't think you will need a single penny more. What happens in reality is that you continue playing the starvation game even after you collect what you require, and there begins a big problem in life. The more you get, the more you need; and life becomes a game of more!

The success is in creation! When you create, the world gets better by using your ideas and creations. Our ancestors gifted us the philosophy of life, knowledge of various areas of life such as medicines, communication, food and many other key things required in daily life. They did not ask for anything in return for this knowledge. They shared it with us because of their love for humanity and the existence of the world.

If you carefully observe, creation spreads across the planet and helps everyone. The collection gets together at one location from various places of the planet. Once the collector changes, the location of the collection also shifts and it never benefits the planet. The collection is always in the custody of someone, without utilisation for years and years when it is most required. Therefore, collecting is against the sustainability of planet earth."

Almost convinced by the philosophy, Ryan had one more doubt. Who cares? It is my choice whether to create or collect and I have complete freedom to choose my way of life. I would rather be happy with a rich but short life. At the end of the day, it's up to me. Why should I even care about the planet when no one cares about me?

The voice explained, "We all have to go back to God after completing our life on planet earth. The very place from where we started our journey. There we will be asked two questions. 'What have you created in your life?' and 'How was your experience with life?' If you have answers to these two questions, your life was truly successful and complete."

As the voice stopped, Ryan got up. It was a fresh Monday morning and Ryan was completely energised and refreshed with the new understanding he'd received last night from the unknown voice. Ryan was still curious about the source of the voice, but he decided not to think about it as he'd already received all his answers and was ready to restart his life with this new philosophy of happiness and fulfilment.

Most of us are like Ryan with similar questions about life left unanswered and buried deep within our minds. As we don't get these answers, we keep living the mediocre life, surrendering ourselves to our self-image of limitations and helplessness. Society further adds fuel to it with its own benchmarks for success which are expected from us to be fit for living. I invite you to the new approach of creation verses collection which can ensure your happiness as well as the sustainability of the planet, so that you get the best experience out of this life and also create something in the process, by which this planet gets better.

I leave it to you to ponder on these thoughts. To make your thinking process easy, I have prepared the following questionnaire for your quick reference, which I hope will be useful to prioritise your actions, enjoy life and be more creative.

Think and write your answers to each of the questions in the following table:

	Life Experience	**Creation**
Your life so far	Did you enjoy it to the fullest?	What did you create for others?
Your plans for the future	Are you hopeful that it is going to make you happy?	Do you think you are going to create something in the process?
Your material possessions	Do you enjoy the process of collection of material possessions? Do you think it is inadequate and you need more to make yourself truly happy?	Do you think you can contribute something to society from the possessions you already have?
Actions to take	What are your 5 key actions from today to enhance your experience in life?	What are your 5 key actions from today to create something and support this planet?

THE TRUE INDEPENDENCE

Every human has four endowments–self-awareness, conscience, independent will and creative imagination. These give us the ultimate human freedom–The power to choose, to respond, to change

– Stephen Covey

One of the most amazing people in my life is my grandmother. She is my guide, mentor, inspiration, motivation and one of the key people who help me develop my philosophy. As I write this book, she is young and enthusiastic in her 90s, helping thousands and thousands of people practice yoga. She has been a yoga practitioner for the past 40 years and after the demise of my grandfather, she has completely devoted her life to a yoga institute. She wakes up at 5 am, conducts her morning yoga classes and looks after the patients who come to the Institute for treatment and therapies all day. Her day ends with evening yoga classes, meditation, music and playing with the children of the staff members residing within the institute. I love visiting her place whenever I get the chance. I often talk to her about my writings and approach to life and she listens to every detail. I really feel blessed to have such a wonderful grandmother.

During one of our conversations, she asked me, "Tell me, what are the most important factors for the failure?"

I thought for a minute and replied, "Fear, assumptions from past experience, lack of consistency in our routines, unhealthy habits, poor health, laziness, ignorance, dependency on approval from others, emotional attachment to goals, financial insecurity, giving up without enough try, reacting before understanding, having the wrong philosophy about life, lack of ability to deal with the negatives in life. Am I right, Granny?"

She smiled and said, "Yes, you are right. You have listed most of the reasons for failure in life. But listen to me, there is only one principle which takes care of everything." I was curious, "Really? And what is that?" Granny continued, "Independence! It is the most important principle in life which governs our happiness. All sorrows of life come from our dependency on something and therefore it is important to achieve true independence in life."

I was now extremely eager to know more about this 'Independence' and I requested Granny to explain to me how to achieve it. Granny continued, "There are three key areas of life from where failure originates: health issues, emotional weakness and financial problems. The one who can control these three areas becomes happy and successful in life. It is important to direct all our efforts to achieve independence in these areas." I was listening carefully. She continued to explain to me, "Now, let's discuss these three areas one by one:

1. **Health Independence:** There is an old saying, 'health is wealth'. If you lose health, you lose the game. Health issues create limitations and it is one of the major reasons for sorrow in today's world. I talk to patients every day and they tell me about the abundance of money they have achieved in their life at the cost of their health. When they come to this institute, they realise the importance of it. But then it is too late, so they

live with medications and permanent limitations for the rest of their life. So, what is the point in having an abundance of money when you cannot enjoy it?

Health independence means maintaining fitness and physical strength by following the right amount of exercise and a healthy diet as a routine. There should not be a dependency on any medication. It is fine if you fall sick once in a while and take medicines to get back to normalcy. However, there should not be a situation where you cannot be normal without medicines.

Again, there could be some cases of health issues by birth or hereditary problems and in those cases, it might be required to take medications regularly. Other than that, you need to maintain your routine in such a way that your day to day life is independent of medicines. There are a number of doctors, knowledge resources, good books on health available today. If you have determination, you can understand the various aspects of human health and customise your diet and physical exercise patterns suitable for your body type and lifestyle and maintain your physical fitness in any situation and any season.

When I talk to my patients, they give me so many excuses for not getting enough time for exercise, but tell me something, do you stop your car for fuelling or continue your journey without fuel just to reach your destination early? Of course, you have to fuel and maintain your car regularly to make good use of it. The same applies to our health as well. People often ignore health under the impression that everything is fine, but they realise when some health issue suddenly hits them, that it is not. The amount of time you spend in a hospital is definitely more than the time you need to spend on exercise every day. When it comes to health, prevention is always better than cure. I hope you understood the importance of Health Independence. Now, let's move on to the emotional aspects of our life.

2. Emotional Independence: I meet with many people in this institute. Every month a new batch of practitioners and patients visit this place. During the open house session, most of them complain that they have difficulty in being calm and peaceful. They are always disturbed by thoughts and incomplete tasks. They are continuously under stress. They think negatively, talk negatively and spread the negativity all the time. They are always complaining about something or the other.

You suggest a solution and they have the perfect answer with a list of examples for why it won't work. They are always diving deep down in the black sea of negativity and just don't want to come out of it. It seems that they are acclimatised to the negative environment. There are some people who make decisions based on their emotional status at the time or their so-called 'mood' at that moment. Now, how can they ensure whether the decision is right when it is left for the mood to manage?

I see people who are overwhelmed by success and shattered by failure. They act like a machine whose controls are in someone else's hand. Someone can decide the reactions and emotions of this machine at any given time by saying just a few words. Now tell me, if your actions are controlled by emotions, how can I expect you to succeed in any field of life?

This kind of dependency on emotions becomes the major reason for a person's vulnerability to failure. You need to be composed, fulfilled, calm, stable and have control over your emotions all the time. Like your body needs physical fitness, your mind needs mental fitness and exercise. The mental exercises are prayers, meditation, adopting a positive attitude about life, helping others, working with a team, spending quality time with your loved ones, practising your hobbies, loving what you do, planning and completing things on time. Also, reading great books and biographies of great personalities, watching inspirational videos and having conversations with people who have a positive attitude towards life can boost your mental fitness. I hope you are getting more clarity as I am covering these key areas. Are you with me?"

I said, "Yes granny, absolutely! I can relate to it." Granny smiled, "That's nice. So, let's move to the next one."

3. **Financial Independence:** This is the third important area which can jeopardise a person if ignored. We all need basic things like food, home and other regular things which are required for our day to day life. We also need to have enough money to sustain any emergency requirements, to have the ability to protect and take care of our family and to support others when they need our help. If we ignore this area, everything gets shattered and goes out of control.

We need to be very clear of our requirements and our capacity to earn. When you earn less than your requirements or when you increase your requirements way beyond your capacity to earn, you invite trouble. Firstly, you need to try reducing your requirements so that you know the things which cannot be avoided. Secondly, you need to find opportunities to save the excess money safely so that emergency requirements will be taken care of. Thirdly, you need to continuously develop and enhance your ability so that you can create more value in the marketplace and increase your rewards. If you take care of these aspects, you are less likely to face financial issues.

Financial independence is the stage where you develop yourself in such a way that you can earn in any situation, save in any situation, spend whenever required and also have enough ability to help others. People with multiple skills can have multiple sources of income and they are less vulnerable to the fluctuations of the market conditions. If one area fails, the income from the other areas will help them. One of the keys here is to increase your abilities and become more valuable. I hope you are now clear on these three areas of life; health independence, emotional independence and financial independence."

As Granny completed, I asked her, "Wow, Granny your knowledge has no limits. You know so many areas of life. I am now clear on what is important in life, but I am not yet sure about how you create balance. I mean, it is highly likely that you just focus on one area and lose control of other areas. For example, you can just focus on your health and emotional aspects and not give enough time to develop your professional skills, which may affect your finances and damage your state of happiness and health."

Granny was happy with the questions. "Great question! Balance is the prime thing. It is difficult but not impossible to achieve. To make you understand it better, I will explain you two scenarios of the lifecycle of Progress and Cycle of Failure.

1. Cycle of Progress: The cycle of progress gives a positive direction to life. Good health supports the mindset, which in turn results in better decisions and better self-control. This helps to gain more capabilities, and we become a more valuable person. A more valuable person can enjoy financial progress.

When we have all three parameters in our control then life becomes enjoyable and successful. Therefore, you need to take care of each of these three areas all the time. The moment you ignore any of them, the progress slows down. Let's consider the other situation.

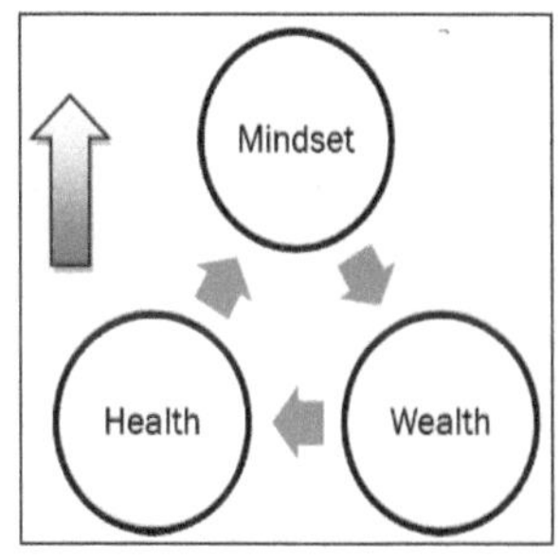

2. The cycle of Failure: The cycle of failure gets triggered when you start ignoring any of the three areas. As you ignore the development of the emotional area, the mindset gets weaker and affects all your thinking and actions. Due to lack of motivation, you lose control of your routine and rituals, which impacts your health.

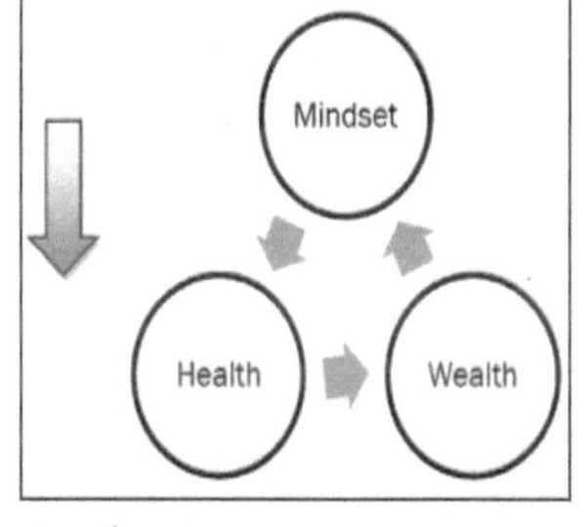

Once you lose control of health and mindset, it also impacts your ability to develop yourself and slowly impacts your capacity to earn. This is how the cycle of failure starts.

I hope you now understand how the balance is important here. If you start ignoring any area, you will soon start experiencing issues with other areas as well. It is absolutely necessary to continuously strive to maintain a balanced lifestyle, so that all of these areas are under your control and you are always in a cycle of progress. The key to success is in balancing the three areas by gathering required knowledge about these areas, developing the rituals for each area, discipline, consistency and regular monitoring of the progress."

I was stunned by the explanation given by Granny. She was so clear about how things work, how we generally lose control of our own progress and blame circumstances for our problems instead of identifying and fixing them.

SUPER ILLUSION OF SUCCESS

Don't wish it were easier; wish you were better

– Jim Rohn

It has been more than 15 years since we graduated. 'The class of 2000' was the most talented batch in the history of the institute. As expected, we were all placed in the best organisations around the world, to begin our career journies with. More than 50 alumni turned up for the reunion at the institute. From young CEOs to business analysts to owners of billionaire brands, the happy and sparkling faces were visible all around, creating a charismatic environment in the hall. They were enthusiastic about sharing their experience.

"Attention! Attention please!" All of a sudden, there was silence as everyone looked at the stage. Aditya, the CEO of a reputed firm, wanted to share something with his mates.

"Did you observe something unique in this hall of fame today?" Everyone looked at each other, clueless. "There is one common thing that almost everyone mentioned in their speech. Most of us have a common measure of success and that is our capacity to accumulate the wealth. But my dear friends, please listen carefully to what I am going to share with you today."

The crowd quietly listened to Aditya, with interest and curiosity. He continued, "Dear friends, I agree that we need wealth to customise our lifestyle, to secure and protect our family, to ensure the sustainability of next generations and to have the freedom to enjoy the journey through life. But in my opinion, this is not the only parameter of success. You all agree on the fact that we worked hard to get into this institute and to survive here. We also put tremendous effort to ensure our success in getting on the right career path and here we are today, enjoying the fruits of our hard work over those years. But if you carefully analyse the situation, you will realise that something was driving us during those years of hard work. Something which kept us motivated to push through the tides and fuelled us. I think that was one of the most important factors for our success. Today, whatever position we are at, whatever work we do and the responsibilities we handle, we still are driven by a passion that keeps us moving ahead. I am sure you all will agree that we will need this 'something' in the future as well.

Society looks at us as an example of success. I get phone calls from my relatives and friends telling me their children want to be like me, get into the same institute, work in the same organisation, dress like me, drive the same car that I drive, live the lifestyle I enjoy and everything else. I am sure you get such calls from your friends and connections as well. When I discussed with their children about their plans and goals, I was surprised to know that they all talk about cars, houses, luxury and a comfortable lifestyle. All of them think that these are the indicators of success.

I am worried about the fact that our societies are creating these benchmarks of success. I mean, you and I know what it takes to maintain our positions and lifestyles. We can do it because we have nurtured and built our own capabilities over the years which enable and empower us to do the work we do today. For us, the 'something' is not only our lifestyle, but we are so confident about our capabilities that they drive us to do the things which society thinks are impossible and unimaginable. With our skills and abilities, we bring great value to the marketplace and hence get rewarded."

As he paused, someone asked him, "But Aditya, what do you think we should do about this? I mean, it is their perception and not our fault. They need to change their way of thinking and we cannot help the perceptions of the society, which are largely driven by comparisons, news, media, marketing and other things they experience in their day to day life. At the most, we can guide the people who are in touch with us, but again there is no guarantee that they will listen to us." Some other members also supported this view.

Aditya explained, "Absolutely. What you say is correct and it is not easy to change society's perception. But I feel a big pain deep within me when I realise that by not doing anything, we are misguiding the society. We are brought up in the same society and are an inseparable part of it even when we are at these positions. Therefore, we have the responsibility to give something back to society. And at this moment, what society needs most is the tool to break this 'super illusion of success'. The basic reason for this illusion lies in blindly following someone, comparing yourself with others and trying to achieve success by short routes. The person who is born rich tends to enjoy the fruits of richness without bothering about hard work because there is no need to work hard, there is no drive. So, the person is born successful."

There was laughter in the hall with this sentence. "Yes, you can see this scenario in today's society. There is a killer competition to show off your capability and standards to the society to earn respect. No matter how you earn it, you need to raise your income levels and show it off to everyone. But what happens is, this mindset removes the drive to learn, to be capable, to uplift the self, to work hard and to help others.

So friends, we need to impart this new mindset to the society and break this super illusion of success. Whenever we talk to our connections, make them understand that success is not in money and material possessions but in being capable, doing your part of work and earning the position you think you deserve. It is not about finding the biggest ladder, but it is about being the strongest and most capable of climbing the mountain.

Let this mindset percolate through society at all levels. Let's try to recreate the lost drive in people's minds. Let's ignite minds which will lead to actions. My dear friends, join me to begin the mission from this moment. Everyone please stand and join me to take the pledge today." Everyone joins Aditya.

"I thank this society for supporting me in my journey to success. I will support this society at my best. I will impart the new mindset that success is not defined by the money and material you possess, but by your personal growth, your hard work, your capabilities, your value addition to the marketplace, the number of jobs you create, the number of people you support and the drive within you for reaching the next milestone. Success is not a milestone where you can rest. Success is a journey which motivates and guides others to find their right tracks and do the hard work necessary to reach there. I will help society in every possible way to come out of the super illusion of success and to develop this new mindset." The hall of fame gets flooded with the claps of the brilliant 'Class of 2000.'

HABITS AND RITUALS

Motivation is what gets you started.
Habit is what keeps you going.

– Jim Rohn

It was a dark night, and we all gathered to experience the meteor shower expected that time. It was also a great opportunity for all of us to capture stunning photographs. Everyone of our team was ready with their high-resolution cameras, advanced telescopes for locating distant objects in space, different lenses, tripods, GPS, timers, and other supporting tech stuff. Everything was perfectly planned based on the calendar of celestial events, geographical coordinates, and other predictive programs. Everyone was excited to experience the meteor shower. That night, we enjoyed photographing the milky-way, star-trail, and the meteor shower. While working, we were discussing the scale of the universe and the many unknown wonders it holds. With the help of technology, we have succeeded in understanding some parts of it and have also realised that there are things beyond our imagination and it is all so huge that we may not even understand its scale with any frame of reference.

It is amazing that there is a systematic arrangement of every object in the universe with some logical reasoning and concepts. These systematic arrangements are operated on a principle of ease and automaticity. Every planet is at a set distance from the Sun and maintains their positions within the defined orbit. Every element of the universe has its own way of operating, its own habits and rituals followed consistently. They have their own set of rules, processes and protocols followed by planets, stars, galaxies and other objects of the universe, making the whole system independent, consistent and efficient. We all know that the gravitational force keeps everything pulled together on earth. When it comes to earth, gravity is the driving force, gravity is the rule and gravity is the ritual. It does not change with situation, season or place and therefore there is a certainty to life on earth, the only known planet supporting life.

The rituals can make a big difference in our lives too. Some of the best-known success stories have become possible because of the consistently followed rituals and habits behind it. If you talk to successful people from various fields, you may find a common trait in all of them. They follow a certain pattern, they make it disciplined, they strive for it and they dedicate themselves to it. Something magical happens when you follow rituals. One of my friends, an athlete, says "I can give at least three important reasons why you should follow rituals:

1. You can rely on yourself
2. Others can rely on you
3. You can create certainty in your life, instead of seeking it from the outside world.

These three things can take your life to a completely new level of success and happiness."

I also have some rituals in my life to help me be more productive and successful. Let's look at some of the rituals which have always helped me:

1. Exercise – Gives vitality and radiant health;
2. Reading – Motivates, educates;
3. Writing – helps to know me, express myself;
4. Prayers – empower my beliefs and give hope;
5. Diet – provides right nutrition and energy;
6. Planning – sets the focus;
7. Meditation – provides mental peace and clarity of thoughts;

I do not forcefully try to fit all of these rituals in my everyday calendar. That is not the point here. There are some things that when followed every day, gives great results, like exercise, diet, prayers and meditation. I keep reading and writing usually on the weekends, other holidays and sometimes during travel. Basically, I select all the things which are critical to my personal and professional life. I select those things which I simply cannot afford to ignore. I have discussed planning in a separate chapter of this book as it is an important area. It is a good practice to list everything together and then prioritise according to your objectives. The first important thing is to act on it. Second, to keep it up consistently and third, to review your list and revise it as necessary, once in a while.

Our habits work both ways. Sometimes, they support our rituals, sometimes they break it. We are sandwiched between the good and bad habits. When it comes to habits, it's a "we know it all, but we still cannot" game. Look at these scenarios:

An apple a day keeps the doctor away! – I eat, on the days I read this message, but soon forget.

Health is wealth! – I exercise for some days when I get inspired by an article about health and after a few days, that inspiration disappears into thin air.

Smoking Kills! – I quit until my friend laughs at me and offers me a cigarette.

Junk food spoils one's health! – I stay away until I see almost everyone is enjoying it and then I tell myself, "Why to think so much? Let's go for it." I know it all, but I am helpless. I decide, I start, I practice it strictly until something hypnotises me and I quit before I realise it.

Knowingly or unknowingly, we all are victims of negative habits at some point in our lives. In spite of our knowledge and experience, we often tend to get trapped into it. Why do we fall into negative habits? Well, habits are just like fillers which fill empty spaces. Our subconscious mind constantly seeks fulfilment in each and everything we do. It is incapable of differentiating between good and bad. It just keeps looking for some filler to occupy the empty space. These fillers, over time, become our routine and stay with us as habits until we consciously force them out of our lifestyle. The selection is strictly on the basis of 'first come, first serve.' Unfortunately, we are surrounded by hundreds of negative things and it is easy to get trapped in negative habits. Despite all available choice and freedom, most of us fall prey!

There can be a whole list of things-to-do to nurture and maintain good habits. However, I personally feel it is more important to follow certain rules to keep you from negative habits. The good news is that you can get rid of it by following simple things in life. All it takes is a few tricks and a new way to look at it. Simple changes in your everyday rituals and adopting a different viewpoint to look at your habits can radically change them. Once you get this right, you will never fall into a bad habit. Here are some effective ways to get rid of negative habits:

1. **Increase your activity levels:** An active lifestyle keeps us healthy and happy. It is a fulfilling experience in itself. When you feel content, you are less likely to get involved in negative habits. I have seen people from all walks of life, from farmers to CEOs, with healthy lifestyles, who are successful in staying away from negative habits. They are self-motivated and focused on the important things in life. There is hardly any space for a bad habit to get in.
2. **Replace it with a good habit:** Typically, bad habits are caught when you spend time with it. Instead, spend your time with good things you always dreamed of. Keep yourself occupied with things you love doing and there will be no time left for the bad habits to get installed into your routine. Replace worrying with creative thinking and helping someone. Replace watching TV and texting on mobile with happy discussion and fun on the dinner table with family and friends. Replace junk food with lots of healthy options, do your research and find options which suit your liking.
3. **Understand the silent damage:** A bad habit can have a significantly negative impact on several areas of our life. Once we analyse and understand the damage it is causing, we will start directing our efforts towards getting rid of it. My friend Diya, used to watch a lot of movies. She loved the experience of having chips and cold drinks while watching movies. Over the years,

she lost her appetite and taste for the common food prepared at home and she relied more on the sugary and salty junk food. Eventually, it became so bad that she lost her physical fitness and the normal health she enjoyed before. It was too late when she realised the overall damage caused by her unhealthy habits. She had to undergo intensive medical treatment and lost important years of her life.

4. **Hate it:** when you hate it, you try to keep yourself away from it consciously. You will also put all your effort into making sure it does not capture you again. When you hate something, your mind spontaneously responds against it. You can use this feeling to keep yourself away from the trap of negative habits. The world champion, Bruce Lee, practised the power of focus. He called it 'laser-like focus.' He hated all distractions to his focus and that's how he trained his mind to be very particular about choosing habits.
5. **Remember, every negative habit is a great salesperson**: Imagine a salesman who comes with his great offers to influence the customers. He uses all possible ways to convince you with the benefits of his product, why you should buy it, how you can use it and how it will give you quick happiness and so on. Similarly, the negative habits come with the great determination to convince you until you buy it. Do not forget you are paying a hefty price for it.

The great leaders, scientists, business creators, mentors, saints, and successful people have one thing in common. They follow a unique protocol to stay away from negative habits. It does not matter where you are, who you are, what profession you are in, what circumstances you are exposed to. The only thing that matters is your conscious efforts to adopt the right habits for your consistent progress towards a successful and fulfilled life.

WHAT'S IN IT FOR ME?

Only those who have learned the power of sincere and selfless contribution experience life's deepest joy: true fulfilment.

– Tony Robbins

What's in it for me? The most frequent question, we ask ourselves every now and then. At home, at the workplace, in social life, even in the wilderness, this question pops up in our mind almost every time. Even as you are reading this book, right at this moment, you are carrying this question on your mind. "What's there in this section of the book for me?" Well, this chapter will help you identify a common answer to this mind-bugging question by understanding a bigger perspective to look at it.

Imagine you are running a marathon. As you complete each mile, you get awarded with a gold medal. Strange, right? You may say people get awards for extraordinary performances and contributions, climbing the Mount Everest, Winning the Formula-1, swimming against the powerful waves of the ocean, hitting a goal against the world's top soccer team, solving the most complicated puzzle, or doing something different, something amazing that has never been done. The award is not meaningful unless the achievement is really significant.

You might think that I am trying to motivate you to work hard to achieve gold medals in life. Not really! There is a very important aspect of motivation that I am trying to portray here. When we do it for a reward, we do our best. We go beyond our limits and try for it. When we know about the reward of completing a task, we make sure to do it effectively to achieve the reward.

The motivation comes from our desire to get rewarded. Bigger the reward, greater is the motivation. But life does not bring you gold medals all the time. There are so many things we need to do without any reward. When there is no reward, we do not want to begin with the task, we do not feel motivated enough. Then we start seeking that missing motivation from somewhere else. We drift in the quest of finding that motivation. Eventually, we get into procrastination mode and keep things incomplete. This gets worse when we start feeling demotivated and depressed. We start hating our job because it is not exciting enough. Believing that changing jobs will solve the problem, we shift places. But the problem still persists and it keeps on haunting us after the initial days of excitement at every new job. The cycle continues, keeping us unhappy all the time. The question remains unanswered, *what's in it for me?*

I remember an instance when I was working on a watercolour painting. I was so involved in the task that I forgot the time. I did not realise that I was hungry until I completed the painting. I was completely connected with the painting process. In the end, I was happy not only with the result but also with the experience. I felt as if I was talking to my work for several hours. I was connected with my painting. I am not a commercial artist. No one was going to reward me for this painting. But I knew there was a hidden reward in the task.

The joy of connection with the task, the involvement in the task and the satisfaction from achieving the desired results. It is very important to understand the fact that there is constant communication between you and your task. The better the communication, the more the connection and you enjoy the process of its execution. When you enjoy the process, you feel excited about doing it, you feel accomplished. This feeling keeps you motivated to take more difficult and challenging tasks. This process helps you grow, get better and better every day. When you strive to establish a connection with every task you do, you connect with it easily and you execute it effectively. You find it meaningful and rewarding. And that is your gold medal in it.

You may be thinking, *What if I do not like my task?* Well, I would say that the liking comes from the connection between you and your task. Unless you try to establish this connection, you will not understand the importance of your task and you will not get a sense of contribution. *What if the task is unimportant or too small?* Remember, if it is not important, it is not a task! The very reason you have the task on your list is that it is important. Each task is a miniature part of a bigger task, a bigger project, and a bigger purpose. So ultimately, you are a part of the bigger purpose. Now, the key here is to establish a connection with that ultimate purpose. How do you do this? Ask the right questions and you will find it! Every task on your list must be associated with its bigger purpose. If you are not clear about that purpose, ask the right questions to the right people and try to find it out. It depends on the source of the task. If you receive a task from your boss, then it is a good idea to ask him about the importance of the task. The earlier you gather these answers, the quicker you connect to the task. We spend the most productive and energetic time of our day at our workplace. As we go through the day, the tasks just keep piling up. Most often, they come without an option of rejecting or complaining or avoiding it. Next time, when you are assigned to a task, instead of trying to get rid of it, try to connect with it. Establishing a good connection with the task makes it enjoyable, meaningful and rewarding – as good as receiving a gold medal for every task you complete.

TIME INVESTMENT

You may delay, but time will not.

– Benjamin Franklin

In our day to day life, we talk a lot about productivity, efficiency, to-do lists, planners, time management and other such buzzwords related to planning and management of tasks and time. We are constantly finding ways to be better in completing tasks, tracking and managing things, both at work and in personal life to be ahead of time. In this quest, we sometimes ignore the actual priorities of life. We just go on cutting the grass linear, acting on those things which come in our way, without thinking much about the rest of the tasks. We give excuses of insufficient time, but this excuse comes out of ignoring our priorities and not being able to allocate time properly. This builds frustration about too many incomplete things in life. It works well to a certain extent, but does not help us achieve our goals. The greater risk is to miss out on critical aspects of goals and dreams in life. When you approach life as it comes, you always experience lack of time. Time is something that is never available enough and seems to run out of our hands all the time. It is a race with time. It's You vs. the Clock. The real tough game! How do we win this game? Running breathlessly behind time is not the solution. I am going to share with you a little different approach here. Instead of trying to fit into the schedule, let's break the schedule. Instead of running behind time, let's ditch the clock! Let's consider these two questions. Do you want to complete the task in given time? Or do you want to spend the minimum possible time to complete it? In the first question 'Time' is the controlling factor, whereas in second question 'You' have the control. You might get the task done even in half the time, it depends on you. The above two questions are our mindsets while we work on the given task. The first question comes from the *time prisoner's* mindset while the second question comes from the *time investor's* mindset. Your mindset determines your victory or defeat in the game. Time is something which is reducing continuously and you cannot regenerate it. The present is constantly flowing out of your basket and becoming your past. When you say there are 20 more years, it means you are going to get just 20 more winters or 20 more summers. That's all! Unlike money, we cannot save time and keep it away for future use. Each moment comes just once in a lifetime and never repeats itself again. There is no second 'second'. It ticks just once.

To solve this puzzle, you need to regulate the usage of the time available to you. You need to invest time wisely. Time investment is based on the principle that the right amount of time spent on the right things is time well invested.

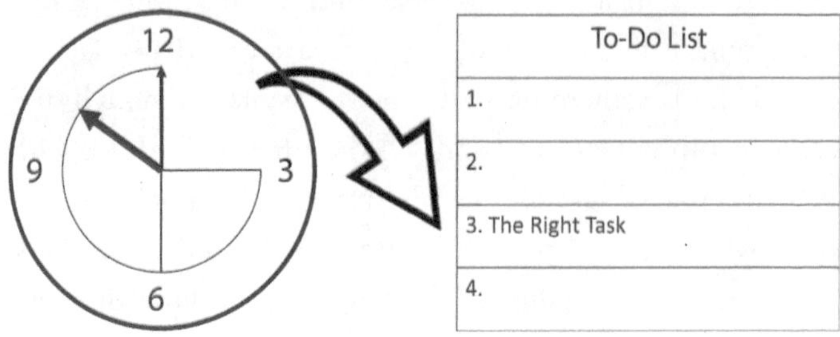

Right amount of time: Here, the 'right amount of time' represents your efficiency, which is totally in your hand. You can enhance it by improving yourself and get more things done in the available time. Here, you need to work on yourself and increase your ability to do things better in lesser time. When your efficiency increases, you save time. You then take control of time instead of running behind the clock.

The right things: The 'right things' are your choices, your selected paths, and your own list of tasks with your own priority definitions. The selection of the right things come from your goals. Now, let's see how we can select the right things. The right things are all the things which are important in achieving your goals and dreams. If you have an urgent task due today, then the related tasks from your to-do list become the right things for you. When you do not have any urgent tasks, you can ask yourself a few questions to identify the right things. Is the task going to help you improve in certain areas? Is the task going to help you in the upcoming projects or things planned ahead? Is it contributing to your 'Internal Income' which is nothing but your personal development, your capabilities, efficiency, and your knowledge? The answer to these questions will help you to identify and prioritise tasks that should be chosen as the right tasks.

There are two famous rules which can help you here:

1. **Rule of 80/20:** This rule says that 80% of your results come from 20% of the tasks. So, you prioritise your task list and identify the important tasks that are linked with 80% of your key results and focus on them. You got your 'Right Things';
2. **Rule of 100%:** This rule says "Be 100% involved in the task you are doing now." Work when you work.

> Play when you play. Do not think about work or some other issue while playing with your kids. Do not think about issues at home when you are at work. Sleep when you sleep, do not think about incomplete tasks of the day. Do not mix both. Try to keep things at their own space and time to the maximum extent possible. Even at the micro level, if you are thinking and worrying about Task-2 while working on Task-1, you are actually not doing any of them. You are not there 100% on either of them, you are in an illusion. And for sure, you are not spending the 'right amount of time' on the task.

Often, we take time for granted. We think time is available in abundance and it is unlimited. But, we forget the very fact that becoming something in the process is more important than just completing the task. Like water takes the shape of the container, tasks tend to expand with the amount of time available. Do not let it. Instead, take your control, spend only the required time on a task and also ensure your personal development through it. Be choosy while selecting the task, be careful while spending your time on the task.

DO NOT LET YOUR PLANS FAIL YOU

Being busy does not always mean real work. The object of all work is production or accomplishment and to either of these ends there must be forethought, system, planning, intelligence, and honest purpose, as well as perspiration. Seeming to do is not doing.

– Thomas A. Edison

Planning is a great tool to get things organised and keep them under our control. We plan all the important things in our life, may it be our personal life or professional life. We plan for various phases of life, long term plans, short term plans, yearly plans, monthly plans, weekly plans, daily plans, and a plan for every hour of the day. We are constantly planning! However, planning alone does not guarantee success. It is our action which sets the sail and determines the quality of results. There is another element between plan and action, which is primarily responsible for converting our plans to action. This third element which plays a critical role in success is "Focus." Eliminate this, and your plans will remain just plans and can never come to reality. It is important to keep yourself focused on current actions and avoid falling prey to distractions. Even our plans distract us sometimes! Yes. You read that right. Our plans can become our distractions. Let's see how it happens.

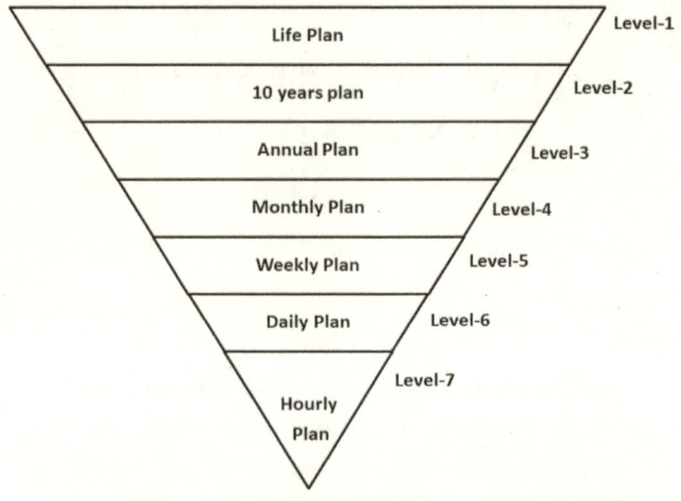

Let's say there are seven levels of plans, from life plan at level-1 to hourly plan at level-7. Ideally, every level feeds to the level below it. Your monthly plan is based on what you want to achieve in a year, likewise your daily plan comes from your weekly objectives, and your hourly plan comes from what you want to achieve that day. All our actions come from the hourly plan and you cannot think of any other level during the execution.

In real life, it is difficult to have everything happening as per your plans from all these levels. And when you face an issue with any of these seven levels, you are concerned about it. You may think about it, worry about it during the action time. If you keep thinking about your life plans or your long terms plans every now and then, it will impact badly on your current actions. Your unhappiness or excitement about long-term plans may distract you from your focus when you constantly think about it. So, even if you have great plans for your life, you are likely to get distracted by the same.

How to deal with such internal distractions? Stop Planning? Or stop thinking? I am presenting here a simple technique which can help you avoid distractions, monitor and implement all your plans effectively. This technique helps to plan well and focus on current actions. As illustrated below, you can set the frequency of reviewing or monitoring your plans within a certain period of time depending on its level. Since your action comes from the hourly plan, do not think about any other plans during that action hour. It may be less than an hour or more, in your case, but the point is to focus only on the current action. Likewise, don't think about your daily to-do list all day, just take one task at a time and complete it. The weekly plan should be reviewed once every day so that you know the status of your progress and identify any additional measures required. In the same way you can set the frequency for all the levels as illustrated in the image here.

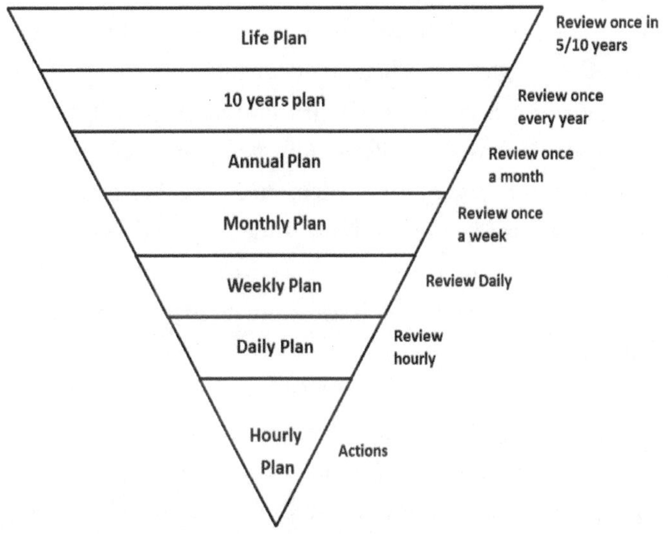

Now, you might be thinking that all this is overly simplistic and in practical life, we have hundreds of different things to do and stringent timelines to follow and this technique may not work. Your thought is absolutely logical. I suggest you choose a specific area of your life and apply this technique for a month as a trial and see the results. You need to use different sheets in the above format for different areas of life. You can also prepare a tracking sheet with your entire to-do list categorised as long and short-term plans. It is also a good idea to transfer all your milestones on a digital calendar and set reminders, so that you don't forget any of them. You can use any method of your convenience and organise all your tasks using this technique.

The idea here is to track the progress of all our plans at the right frequency and stop getting distracted by our own dreams and plans. It is easy to forget about some of our plans as we get busy in our daily routine and changes in our priorities. We also have very limited control over our circumstances and sometimes have to deal with unforeseen things in life and lose track of the predefined schedule. It catches us at some point in time and we feel frustrated about those incomplete tasks and unfulfilled dreams. Our life is full of unpredictable ups and downs and our state of mind keeps changing. We make plans when we are most excited about something and later betray them when the ride is rough and we feel unexcited. The best way to keep our plans alive is to automate them with the help of an independent system.

For your ready reference, I am providing you with the sample template here. Take one project at a time, try this technique, get rid of distractions, focus on your actions and monitor your plans only when you get a reminder from your automated system. Get productive, be happy.

Track Your Top-5 To-Dos

To be Reviewed	To-Dos
Once in 10 Years	- - - -
Once in 5 Years	- - - -
Yearly	- - - -
Monthly	- - - -
Weekly	- - - -
Daily	- - - -

SELF-IMAGE AND PUBLIC-IMAGE

You can fool some of the people all of the time, and all of the people some of the time, but you cannot fool all of the people all of the time.

– Abraham Lincoln

This is the story of a Queen who loved the fragrance of fresh flowers sent by the flower merchant every morning to her palace. Her day started with the basket of fresh flowers. The Queen was happy with the flowers and appreciated the flower merchant with rewards. He became the richest flower merchant in the town. One fine day, out of curiosity, the Queen decided to visit the garden from where these flowers are picked up every morning. Upon arriving at the garden, she felt like it was heaven—full of beautiful flowers and their magical fragrance. The Queen was very impressed with the artistic arrangement of the garden. She thought the flower merchant was the person who'd created the garden and gifted him a bag of gold coins as a token of appreciation. But her happiness was shattered the moment she saw a dirty old man working in the garden. He offered greetings to the Queen, but she was irritated with his dirty clothes, the sweat on his face and his ugliness. Without much thought, she reacted "Who is this dirty man? I don't want such ugliness in our beautiful kingdom. I want this dirt to be thrown out of our kingdom. I don't want to see this face again." The servants could not change her mind and had to follow the orders.

Within a few days, the fragrance from the basket of flowers changed. The flower merchant, with a new gardener, could not manage to get the same quality of flowers as before. The Queen was disappointed with this change and asked the merchant about the problem. The merchant presents various excuses, including lack of rain, bad season, too much wind, and new insects, just to convince the Queen. The merchant gets money to repair and renew the garden with the fresh plantation. As a new responsibility and additional workload, he also gets another bag of gold coins. Looking at the sad face of the merchant, the Queen further decides that she will help the merchant for any financial problems he might face in his job. The rich merchant gets richer and richer using his tactics. Months slip into years. The Queen keeps on dreaming about the basket of flowers and the magical fragrance, but never gets it. Meanwhile, the old, ugly gardener develops his garden in another kingdom. One fine morning, the Queen receives a basket of flowers with the magical fragrance and freshness she dreamt of. The basket also contained a letter, written by the King of that town with the following message:

"The beautiful diamonds come by the hard work of ugly labourers from the dirty coal mine. The smart merchant talks only about its shine."

The Queen realises her mistake and calls the merchant to her palace, "I want to grow a similar garden in the backyard of this palace. I want you to grow the flowers with the magical fragrance. You will get all the gold you want for this job. Start the work from tomorrow." The merchant was trapped. He didn't know what to say. He knew very well that he was unable to do this. He tried giving reasons for why it was not a good idea to grow a garden here, "Your Highness, it is not a good season to grow the garden. Also, the place is not suitable for it. There will be so many workers in the garden, disturbing the peace of this area around the palace. You will also get a lot of insects due to the flowers. So, I suggest you reconsider your plans."

The Queen smiled, "Dear merchant, I am okay with all those problems. I want you to start the work immediately." The merchant was now afraid. He realised that it was his only chance to surrender and accept the mistake, "Your Highness, please forgive me. I accept my mistake. I did the wrong thing. I betrayed you. I lied. I did this to get more money and gold. I was just thinking about collecting. Actually, I don't have any skills to grow the garden. It was only possible because of the knowledge and hard work of the old gardener. I always lied to you to get the benefits. I am sorry for what I did."

The Queen gets disappointed by hearing all this, "It's good that you accepted your mistake. You still deserve punishment for your behaviour. Soldiers, send this person to prison immediately. His punishment will be decided during the next assembly."

It is very common to get impressed by the external characteristics than understanding the internal world. We normally believe what we see, which may however be very different than the facts. So, my internal self is different from my external self. My internal self is what I know I am or what I believe I am. This forms our self-image. The external self is what others think I am. This is largely defined by my public-image. In our story, the merchant projected a false public-image to fool everyone and get benefits. We must note that he was successful in that and he got what he wanted till the time he was caught. These two images play crucial roles in our happiness and success. They define and shape our personality. They drive our thought processes and direct our actions. Therefore, our success and failure first get formed in these images before getting into reality.

Self-Image: The self-image is what we carry with us everywhere. It is our understanding and impression of ourselves, our capabilities and limitations. In fact, our choices, our expectations, our lifestyle, motivation, inspiration, hopes, spirituality and our overall personal growth are directly linked with our self-image.

Public-Image: The public-image is what we project about ourselves, knowingly or unknowingly, to the external world. It is our image as perceived by others. It starts with the first impression and gets framed as you interact with others. Public-image is other's understanding about you, your capabilities, weaknesses and your nature. The way people behave with you is determined by this image. Therefore, the public image has a direct relationship with your success and failure. Now, it is very interesting to see how these two images have the power to make or break us. For that, let's understand the various scenarios, their characteristics and how they work. I would like to highlight the four key categories based on the various personality types we see:

1. ***Weak SI, Strong PI:*** In this case, the person knows about his weaknesses and lack of certain skills, but still projects himself intelligently and manages to create a strong public image. Just like the flower merchant in our story. The person feels great and enjoys the success achieved this way. However, the major risk remains with him. He never realises this trap. He never feels the requirement of improving the SI. And suddenly, when the PI gets the hit, the person collapses. Many of us walk the path with the support of PI. We climb the ladder for the sake of it, but what is the point in such success when you are hollow from the inside. With a weak SI, we remain a loser even though we win. Such a sad life!
2. ***Strong SI, Weak PI:*** People under this category possess the required skills and they are confident about it. However, they do not project it to the world. They do not care about their public image. Only if you know them closely, you know what they really are. Otherwise, the chances are that you have the wrong impression of these people. Remember the old gardener from our story? That's the case here. He knew about his skills, but never projected it. The Queen perceived a false image about him and that made him struggle. The logic is simple, if you don't work on our public image, it will get created anyway, but you do not know what it is. Instead, if we consciously work on it, we can define our public image. This is a very important aspect of our personal growth. Who has the time and interest to analyse you in detail every single time? It is our responsibility

to work on our public image. As people know you more, they can easily see the gap between your SI and PI, and this is where the trust factor gets developed. More gaps they see, lesser they trust you.

3. ***Weak SI, Weak PI:*** This category represents failure. People in this category lack the skills and knowledge; even if they have it, they are not confident about it. They underestimate themselves. They are very much attached to their self-image and often seem frustrated with it. Without self-respect, a person cannot succeed in life. They are different from our flower merchant, they do not project themselves deceptively. So, they are basically good-minded people who are lost in themselves so much that they cannot achieve success in life. What is the point in being good when you are not able to support yourself? It also means that you are not able to support others. Moreover, with the weak PI, you are less likely to get support from others. They might just see you as a sad person and that will be your public image.

   This is a dangerous place to be in. If you are in this category, act immediately and get out of this dead zone. Work hard on yourself, do whatever it takes and create a stronger SI. Start interacting with people and understanding people, have quality conversations and develop your public image.

4. ***Strong SI, Strong PI:*** This is the ultimate success zone. People with strong SI and PI are the happiest and most successful in life. They are skilful, confident and people respect them. Even if their PI is attacked, they are not shattered, because their SI tells them,

> "Don't worry, we can build the empire again." And they rise up again and again. These are the people who dream big, deliver miracles, bring reforms, and have their impact on the world. These are the people who set great examples, motivate others and lead the path of progress. They are the real creators and the real contributors of their life.

All our efforts should be focused on setting a mindset that will allow us to develop a strong SI and a strong PI. Here are some tactics that might help:

To develop Strong SI:

- Work on yourself and acquire the necessary skills;
- Develop good health, a better mindset and rituals;
- Know yourself and monitor your own progress regularly;
- Keep learning throughout your life and keep upgrading yourself as necessary;
- Develop your own values and philosophy about life;
- Set objectives and be fuelled and driven to achieve them;
- Convince yourself that you have what it takes to be a successful person;
- Once you are confident about your own capabilities, your performance will reflect that;
- Experience life at its fullest;
- Help others and contribute to society so you never feel regret;
- And most importantly, have gratitude for the things you are blessed with;

To develop Strong PI:

- Help others and contribute to society;
- Walk the talk, keep your commitments;
- Be true and honest with yourself;
- Work on your communication skills and have meaningful conversations;
- Be open to share ideas, get feedback and suggestions from others;
- Respect your connections, make time for them, be there with them when they really need support;
- Spend quality time with your loved ones;
- Share your goals and objectives with others, let them know what you are up to;
- Share your success stories with others;
- Keep consistency in your behaviour and personality traits;
- Build teams and motivate people for a positive change and be with them;
- Share your learning and experience with others;
- Do not criticise others; if possible, help them to get out of that situation instead;
- Create your own brand, let people recognise you for that and value you for that;
- Always work to bring value to the team;
- Be objective oriented, not emotion or mood oriented;
- And most importantly, be a true human being, love and respect everyone around you, be grateful for this life;

The list is endless. But it's important to just pick the right tools and go ahead. Time will never wait for anyone and life is really too short to spend time in the dead zone. Just get up, set the right mindset and start walking the path of true success, a meaningful and joyful life.

PASSION, PURPOSE AND THE GREAT ILLUSION OF MODERN AGE

When you catch a glimpse of your potential, that's when passion is born.

– Zig Ziglar

These days, we talk a lot about finding our purpose and passion. I have, in fact, seen many examples of people changing their careers and shifting to new areas to follow their passion. I support this talk and I am convinced that if you are passionate about your work, you will do your best. However, I would like to highlight another perspective on this subject. There is a difference between being passionate and being knowledgeable about something. Let's take the example of my passion. I am passionate about art. I have taken some online lessons, attended a few art workshops to learn the basics of painting. I love spending hours working on the canvas. Sometimes, I even forget about time and I keep working on it until I get the desired outcome. Most importantly, I don't feel tired while doing this activity. But at the same time, I know the limitations of art and I know what it takes to pursue it as a career option. It's a no-no area for me from a full-time career point of view.

Recently, one of my close friends left his job and started a business of buying and selling used cars. He was always interested in cars, even in our school days. I still remember those late-night group talks in the college campus when he used to share his knowledge about interesting technological features of advanced cars. He was passionate about cars. When I happened to meet with his colleagues from his previous job, I got to know about the other side of his decision. They told me that he never focused on his job, never tried to learn seriously and was a very ignorant person when it came to work. Initially, I thought this was because he was never interested in that career. And this is good enough a reason to leave the job. One day, I thought of talking to him over the phone about his progress in his new business. I was shocked to hear the truth from the horse's mouth. The new venture was not helping his career. With all the passion he had for cars and technology, he was still not able to manage his clients and handle the negotiation meetings. The new business needed management skills which he ignored learning at his earlier job. I asked him about the reason he left the job without properly estimating the risks of his new business line. I was surprised to know that his passion for cars was not the only reason for his resignation. In fact, he used it as an excuse to convince himself to resign. He used to live in dreams about his passion and made it the excuse for every problem he faced in the job. So, he never thought of finding solutions or learning the required skills. Instead, he kept dreaming and waiting for the right time to resign, without even knowing what it takes to start his new business. Now, he was stuck between two career choices. There are many such examples of people getting trapped in a dilemma between passion and career.

He is not the only person facing this situation. I have met so many people struggling on this front. They allow themselves to go into the illusion of following their passion and then the story begins. In many of these cases, people fool themselves by living in the illusion, constantly thinking about an imaginary world where success is waiting for them. They neither focus on their current work nor spend enough time to critically review their plans of following their passion as a career option.

There is no perfect workplace or business that is free of problems. We need to deal with some or the other issue every day at the workplace, no matter what position you are working at. Instead of facing the situation and working towards solutions, if we give up and run away from the situation in the name of our passion and purpose, then we are fooling ourselves and everyone else, including our loved ones. Whatever excuses we make to get rid of work make us weaker and weaker, regarding our abilities to work on it. When we give excuses, we are actually running away from the mainstream and losing the connection with our main track and that's where the trap is. We get into the trap of weakness. Our abilities get diminished due to lack of practice in executing the tasks. Moreover, we get habituated to look for an easy way out from every problem, instead of going through it and fighting it out like a soldier. This whole process makes us weak.

Here you may say, "But we never have choices for some things in life. Then how can we align our interests and our work?" Although, we cannot have choices for everything in life, we should understand our interests and align our education and career choices accordingly. At the same time, we also should keep in mind that there is a difference between liking and knowing. Liking won't take you too far as a career option, but knowing will. Get out of the illusion. Connect your liking with your knowledge and with your career option so that you have more chances of being successful in the area you are venturing into.

The other day, I was talking to a young boy who was confused about his career choices. He said, "I do so many things for my overall improvement, I work hard on studies, I work hard on my physical fitness. One day, I want to make a lot of money and earn respect in society. But I am not sure what the best career choice to fulfil my dreams quicker is. I have seen many people fail and I don't want to get into those careers. Also, the selected field should not be boring for me; otherwise, I may quit half way. Please, can you help me out to select the right career option?" It was challenging for me to guide this boy out of his confusion. I didn't want to tell him straight that there is no such way where everything is quick and certain. I decided to give him some examples, "My dear friend, I understand you. I know what exactly you are talking about. I know what you are going through in this phase. And I have good news for you, there is a way out." The boy was happy to know that I had a solution to his problem.

I continued, "Before we talk about solutions, let's take an example which will make it easy for you to understand the whole concept. Consider that there is a box of ice cream in front of you which has various flavours. You have never tested the ice cream before and there is no way you can test it before you select one of it. You have to select just one out of it without even knowing its colour, texture or size. The only information you have is the main ingredient of each ice cream. Now, tell me how you will select the ice cream."

The boy started thinking. He said, "I will just ask other people which ice cream is better and then make my choice."

"What if you still make the wrong choice?" I asked, to catch him spot on. "I don't know. Maybe that's why I am asking for your help." This made me laugh, "Ha-ha! I knew you were going to say that. But just think about it. You are in a similar situation at this moment of time. You do not have much idea about where a specific career choice can take you. Now, let me first reveal the answer to the ice cream puzzle. Remember, I told you that you have information about the main ingredients of the ice cream? That's the first part of the answer.

The other part of the answer was in your first guess, "asking others". You were partially correct there, but it is important what you ask. Instead of just asking about what ice cream to choose, you should ask them for details about the ingredients, the properties, which one has more value, which ingredient is healthier and how it tastes. You can also collect more information about why people prefer a certain type of ice cream more than the others. You can ask about their experience of having a particular ice cream. With all such information, you can zero-in on your choice and go for it."

The boy was partially convinced. He further asked, "But what if I still do not like the taste? What if they give me wrong advise? What if I get distracted by others' choices and the look in their happy faces?" "That's a great question. This is exactly what will happen after you make your choice. The fact is that, you will never be 100% correct in your selection. You will never have the certainty that you are expecting from life. You will unknowingly compare with others' choices. You are likely to get the wrong advice from people out there who don't want you to succeed. They are stuck in their own negativities and see everything else with a negative vision. You have no control here. All that you can do is research and explore the maximum possible sources of information on a particular subject, which will help you in your decision-making process.

Now, the question still remains. What if you still make the wrong choice? There is nothing perfect in this world. You can make your best plans and estimates, but they will only be predictions about how it may unfold for you. They definitely are useful, but you cannot expect them to be perfect all the time. You still have to do your preparations. You still have to be ready to face whatever comes your way. Sometimes, we spend so much time on our predictions that we lose our main track and our focus. Another problem with prediction is that we unknowingly expect everything to happen accordingly and any deviation from it may frighten us and make us uncomfortable, leaving us frustrated. The most effective way to get out of this trap is to be dynamic. Get the required guidance from planning and from shared experiences, but also learn from people's failures. Many people fail not because of the wrong choices they make, but because of their wrong approach to life.

Remember, you mentioned that your objective is to earn a lot of money and respect in society and that you want it to happen quick and easy? There is nothing wrong with this objective, but just analyse it properly. When your objective is to earn a lot of money, you will probably never get satisfied in life. You can never define how much 'a lot of money' is. You are most likely to get trapped into the 'more and more' race. Try to understand the difference between a lot of money and financial security. It is always better to aim for financial security which gives you freedom and happiness in life. For your information, happiness and satisfaction from life are becoming a rare experience for people these days that some countries are trying to factor in these parameters into the indicator of the national growth rate. The more number of happy and content people means more growth, more progress the country has made in its fiscal department.

Now, let's talk about earning 'respect' in society. This is another deadly trap so many people fall into. We are all a part of the same society and have a similar set of objectives, expectations and nature of problems. When we seek respect from society or approval from others for what we do, we often give control of our happiness to others. If others say that whatever you do is wrong, then you may also feel it is wrong, even when it is not. And most of the time, guess what others would like you to be. I think you have the answer. Never ever do things just to seek others' certification. I have seen some people spend sleepless nights thinking about someone's comment at the previous evening's birthday party that their new house's interiors have the wrong colour choice, or that the new car they purchased is not the best choice. Just think how much impact it can have on your life when you give control to others.

The third point is about the quick and easy way. There is a thumb rule among farmers. The more time it takes to grow, more the time it takes to cook, and more the nutrition it has got. The quick and easy way is not long-lasting and resilient. When you seek quick and easy ways, you lose your ability to handle hard work. You lose the opportunity to get stronger. You lose your chance to get better. The quick and easy way can be done by anybody, leaving more competition for you. But hard things are possible only for those who develop such abilities. So, do not think small, just go for the big, get ready for bigger challenges, get excited about adventures of life and get stronger and better every day.

The biggest mantra of life is that you seek knowledge and you will become powerful, you seek challenges and you will become strong, you seek to get better and you will grow, you seek to contribute and you will become happy, you seek to create something to help planet earth and you will get fulfilment in life."

To my surprise, the boy got up and hugged me tight with tears rolling down his eyes.

WHAT'S YOUR RELIABILITY INDEX

Everything comes to us that belong to us if we create the capacity to receive it.

– Rabindranath Tagore

Everyone wants to be successful in life, irrespective of the type of work they do. When it comes to success and failure, whatever the situation, there are certain factors such as the skillset, mindset, qualification and experience that always play their role. While we all know about these factors, there is an underlying parameter called the reliability index, which in most cases act as the determining factor. Let's see what this reliability index is all about.

The professional relationship between an employer and an employee depends on their individual objectives. Although, these objectives are different, each one is supporting the other party and receiving monetary returns. In other words, an employee gets paid for the value he/she creates for an employer. The employee aims for career development along with financial growth, while the employer looks to leverage the skills of an employee to generate more profits for the firm. In this transaction between the two parties, the one who has less dependency on the other dominates. But if they focus just on dependency, then it may not be a sustainable relationship. It takes a great amount of trust to make it sustainable in the long run. This trust comes from reliability. When an employer sees that the employee is reliable, there is a whole new relationship that develops. The reliable employees get more opportunities, responsibilities and more rewards than others.

The reliability index is the measure of reliability of a person. The more reliable you are, the higher is your reliability index. When it comes to downsizing, companies first check for the employees who have a high reliability index and often retain them. Your value is decided by your reliability index. So, in the time of recession, this one is a lifesaving factor. There are certain parameters which help improve this index, while there are others that damage it. So, it is important to carefully consider these parameters. Let's look into some of these parameters:

Efficiency: This tops the list. It is the ratio of the value you bring to the time you consume in the task. The lesser the time, the more efficient you are. For almost every business, time is the most important commodity. So, being more efficient boosts your reliability index.

Productivity: This is the ratio of the number of completed tasks to the total tasks assigned to you. The more the percentage of completion, higher is your index. In today's competitive world, no business can afford to have more incomplete tasks. Higher productivity means more profits and more potential to expand the business.

Discipline: This parameter defines your public image. This is something that is very visible to others. The disciplined people keep their promises, plan everything in advance and execute it with passion. This helps you to maintain accuracy and precision in the things you do. Any business would want to have minimum mistakes and more accuracy. And guess whom the company would assign the complex jobs to.

Focus: Bruce Lee was obsessed with this term. He used to say, "Laser-like focus." And all his practice was to achieve this. When you are focused, you are less likely to get distracted by unimportant things. More focus means more capability of understanding, which gives you more clarity and better knowledge. More knowledge means better decisions. Just imagine what else a company would want than people with better decision-making skills.

Consistency: "Give me the winter and I would make anything possible, for I do not feel like doing anything in monsoon."

Who would like to employ a person who works well only when he feels like it. Companies are under tremendous pressure of changing market situations and technologies every single day. We all need to be adaptive to change.

Irrespective of the situation, we need to keep going. Inconsistent people cannot develop the reliability.

Character: The character of a person is judged by his behaviour and attitude. It is becoming an important factor in the hiring process of some of the leading organisations these days. The excellent skill set, communication skills and a good character makes the perfect candidate. The person with a good character is dedicated, honest and strong-minded. Such a person is a better decision maker in every situation. The good character influences the team with a positive impact and such a person builds the teamwork culture in the organisation. Such a person can change the brand value of the organisation to a whole new level of repute.

There are many parameters which decide your reliability index. However, the above five are, in my opinion, the key ones. Analyse yourself with these parameters and try to relate to your situation. It may be about your progress in the current organisation or it may be about job uncertainty and the fear of layoff, you will find that the answer lies in the reliability index.

IMPORTANCE OF DEVELOPING THE CULTURE

The bottom line is, when people are crystal clear about the most important priorities of the organisation and team they work with and prioritised their work around those top priorities, not only are they many times more productive, they discover they have the time they need to have a whole life

– Stephen Covey

Every organisation starts with an idea that occurred to a human mind, executed with a certain vision, and developed with a clear policy. It works like a pyramid with a flow of operational strategies from top to bottom and the execution of these strategies typically at the bottom levels. In this flow, it is extremely important that the core vision and policy percolates through all levels, from top to bottom. The fleet at the execution level requires direction and fuel from higher levels to maintain its course. The devil is in the details! It's not always the case that everything from top to bottom percolates with gravity and is well received at the execution house. The communication gaps, differences in opinions, lack of transparency, working style, personal philosophy, level of experience and so many such factors play a silent role and the devil enters the ground. It goes further, takes control over things and creates resistance. The resistance to flow, resistance to succeed. The devil attacks at micro levels, starts eating substantial amounts of time of the organisation in the battle. The main objective of the devil is to keep the battle going and it finds different ways and means to do it. This paralyses the policy, vision and operational capabilities of the system. Being at a micro level, this becomes difficult for organisations to identify and cure. Often, as a first aid measure, organisations try changing and restructuring the teams, which makes no big difference as the devil stays in the system, fused with culture.

The solution usually lies in changing the organisational culture. Though it is not easy to change the culture overnight, the small steps taken towards it, consistently over time, can help make the situation better. The organisation should invest conscious efforts towards this. It is also important to bring them all together under one umbrella. The team should feel connected with each other, they should be aware that they are contributing to a larger objective of the organisation, they should be provided with a clear understanding of how they are progressing with the organisation. The team pours themselves into the work when they are motivated, respected, connected, heard, valued and trained. When they feel like prisoners or slaves, the contribution vanishes. When they are forced, the values are shattered. When they are ignored, they are disconnected. When they do not find a leader, they get mislead. When they are not given direction, they try to push the organisation in any direction they want and effectively, the organisation does not move to the desired direction. It remains standing still and everyone wonders why we're not progressing.

Let's see some of the key parameters which play a significant role in developing a great culture in organisations:

Creating a Common Goal: This is critical and sets the direction of the ship. Things can go wrong if there is a lack of clarity in this area. With the devil's programming, the organisation is fragmented into various teams with their own goals and plans. This pushes the ship in multiple directions and slows it down. Having a common goal clearly conveyed to all levels, can help rebuild the team and get the ship to move forward.

Win-Win Situation: Every successful business transaction is based on creating a win-win situation. All parties involved in it should have their own benefits from the deal. The same applies to the employer and employee relationship. It is important to have effective communication between the top level and bottom level to ensure the win-win situation is maintained, which is the key driver of motivation.

Every Opinion is Important: It helps to have common meetings and open forums to collect opinions from all levels. The sense of accountability comes from being involved and having a say. Every team member is a stakeholder in the progress of the organisation and their involvement is critical to the success of the team.

Branding Together: A casual chat with a co-traveller during a journey can create a potential business opportunity. When branding is done by every single member at their own levels, they need to focus on the good things about the organisation. A sense of ownership is developed when the entire team is involved in the branding of the organisation in some way or the other. Every level can contribute to the branding exercise through various interactions with external parties such as clients, parteners, other stakeholders, media etc. This can be practised as a planned activity with a clear protocol so that the desired message is conveyed.

We are all human beings with the common goal of having a happy and meaningful life. Happiness comes from accomplishments and meaning comes from a sense of ownership and contribution to an important task. It is very crucial for the success of any organisation to design and maintain the in-house culture which motivates the team and creates the path of happiness.

DIET, EXERCISE AND THE HEALTH TRAP

Without health life is not life; it is only a state of languor and suffering - an image of death.

– Buddha

Don't we already know about this? There are many books, websites, training institutes, courses and even friends and relatives who are experts in areas of health and fitness. But we still feel trapped under the pile of information without knowing the what, when, why and how. Is the problem with information? Or is it with us? The answer is a 'no' to both these questions. The problem lies somewhere else. There is an invisible trap which plays a major role in this whole matter. In order to see how this trap is created, what the various factors responsible for it are, and how the trap succeeds in hypnotising us, we need to consider four scenarios in which it operates. These four scenarios provide favourable conditions for the development of this trap. The letter 'E' and 'D' indicates Exercise and Diet respectively.

The symbol '+' and '–' indicates the positive and negative respectively. Let's first define these parameters and then discuss the four scenarios they bring.

E–: Without Exercise: This is the situation when you ignore your exercise routine and go for days without activity. In your mind, you know the importance of your routine, but somehow, you are not able to manage it. So, you get frustrated with it. This again reduces your motivation and inspiration for exercise. It also impacts your diet, as you will crave for favourite food to get out of frustration.

E+: With Exercise: With routine exercise, you will feel motivated and inspired. The happy feeling will also keep you more active and healthy. This also improves your diet, as you won't feel the cravings, and will be more disciplined regarding your health. You will also have a stable mind due to good health. This will help you keep going.

D–: Unhealthy Diet Routine: Unhealthy eating habits spoil the game. It first impacts your health badly and then takes away your energy. You do not feel like exercising. You also are caught by the toxic diet in such a way that you cannot get out of it.

D+: Healthy Diet Routine: This gives you more energy and keeps you active. It helps you to stick to your exercise routine also. You do not crave for junk food. You do not get lazy for exercise. So, you are always motivated and inspired.

Now, just E+ or D+ is not enough. You need to also avoid combinations of E+&D– and E–&D+ as one negative drags down the other positive. Let's see how the four scenarios work.

Scenario-1 (E+ & D–): In this scenario, your exercise routine gets impacted by your unhealthy diet choices. As you are burning calories every day, you don't feel guilty about having junk food occasionally. In addition, you do not count your calorie intake, as you can convince yourself on the basis of your exercise routine every time you eat it. So, you do not realise when this diet takes over and starts impacting your exercise routine. Suddenly, one fine morning, you feel like not waking up early and surprisingly, you find some excuse such as 'I am too tired', 'I could not sleep properly so there is no point doing exercise', 'I have maintained my routine for so many months with great discipline and I deserve at least one break', 'why should I push myself too much for this routine, instead I should take it easy, after all it is about my own happiness, then why should I get stressed about it', 'Just one day is not going to make any difference to my health'. All set, and you are already in the trap. You are slowly moving towards E–&D– scenario.

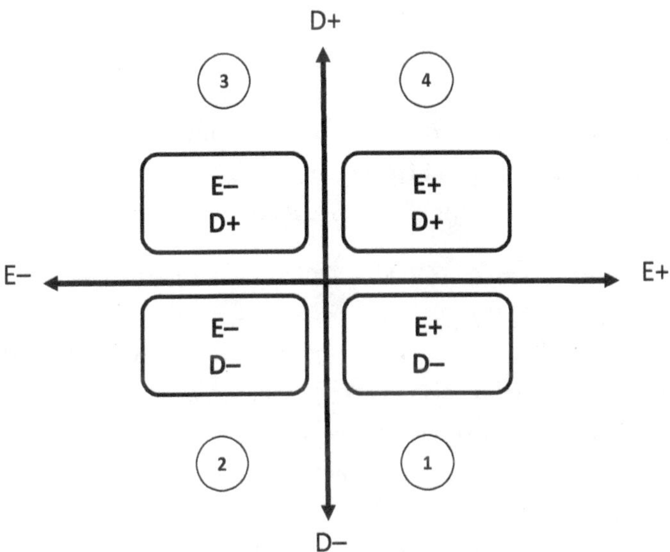

Scenario-2 (E– & D–): This is a total disaster. In this scenario, you act brilliantly and with a completely new set of philosophies, along with a laundry list of excuses to convince yourself for 'why am I not on the right track'. You feel better when you have that junk food or excess food. This helps you feel so comfortable that you don't feel like doing any physical activity. You find an easy way out for each task which needs physical work. You find so many occasions to have delicious food. Food becomes your support to feel happy. You love it so much and no one can separate you from it, not even thoughts about health. The result is a typical mix of procrastination, ignorance and excuses where health is at risk and you slowly slip into the danger zone from the comfort zone.

Scenario-3 (E– & D+): In this case, you are conscious about your diet. You pick the healthy quality and quantity in whatever you eat. You know what is good for you and what is not. You are well disciplined in this area. But you are ignorant about your exercise routine. Without exercise, you may not even know when you will lose your health even if you are maintaining a healthy diet. No exercise leads to a lack of motivation, inner inspiration and a good feeling about life. Slowly, it turns into the risk of you ignoring your diet routine as well.

Scenario-4 (E+ & D+): This should be our normal scenario. You are following the exercise as well as the diet routine properly. Diet and exercise not only keep you motivated and energetic, but also work in synergy and support each other. Effectively, you get great health and a positive outlook toward life, with higher productivity at work. When you are consistent at both E and D, you are at your best. When you are at your best, you can support others at your best to get to their best. While we think about deserving this or that, it is actually E+ & D+ that you deserve the most. You deserve to become great at what you do. You deserve to effectively play your role in life and work. You deserve to feel motivated and also motivate others in your circle. You deserve to get to the mountaintop where your dreams will be fulfilled. You deserve to help humanity. You deserve to make significant contributions towards planet earth and make it a better place for the next generations to come.

Once you identify your scenario, the following section can help you to get unstuck and move to the E+D+ scenario.

Getting out of E+ & D– Scenario: Get out of the lonely road first. Join a group of friends for doing your exercise.

Talk to the people who have better fitness than you. Just spend time with them, take their guidance on improving your diet plans. Understand more about the basics of diet and how they relate to your situation. Remember, when you are here, you are better than others, as the E is already in your control and you are already in action. From here, it is not too far to reach the D+.

Getting out of E– & D– Scenario: This is the most challenging situation. You are stuck between two swords. You need to act like a warrior here. As we discussed how to deal with bad habits in Chapter 5 of this book, you need to hate it. Hate yourself for not doing exercise. Ridicule yourself for not maintaining a simple thing like diet. But in addition to this, you need to act immediately. Get up and hit the gym. Go for long walks with your friends. Find a trainer or mentor in whatever activity you are doing. This mentor will not only train you to do the activity, but also motivate you. When you are stuck here, you really need someone who can motivate you and push you to action. Once you are in action, the next immediate step is to look at your diet. Again, get guidance from your mentor. Talk to him about your problems and he will surely help you out.

Getting out of E– & D+ Scenario: This is not as bad as E–D, but there is still a potential issue. E– is something which is difficult to deal with. It makes you act against your comfort zone when you try to get rid of E–. Again, join the group, find your mentor, get guidance, stop procrastinating and hit the ground right now. Everything is possible when you are in action. A good thing about this situation is that D is already in your control. So, you need to just work on E and protect yourself from slipping into E–D– scenario. You may also apply the flight theory to get unstuck from your current phase. Flight theory is based on the various phases of flight operations and its relation to our life. Let's move to the next chapter to read about it.

THE FLIGHT THEORY

Humans are creatures of habit. If you quit when things get tough, it gets that much easier to quit the next time. On the other hand, if you force yourself to push through it, the grit begins to grow in you.

– Travis Bradberry

All the excitement disappeared within a fraction of a second and was replaced with fear, taking my pulse and breath out of my control. I was shouting out loud with my mouth shut and my voice mute. I wanted desperately to get out of that phase, but the flight's speed was increasing with more vibrations and noises. To add to this, it took a nice bend and turn in the air, showing us tiny houses and river streams from the window, trying to stop my heartbeat.

The take-off drama of my first ever flight experience left me looking like a paralysed person coming out of the hospital. "Are you OK?" my fellow passenger asked looking at my situation. I took some time to think about the answer, "Yes. I am fine. Thank you. Actually, I am flying for the first time. So, I am scared." He smiled, "It happens. I take it as a test of my faith in God. I cannot be afraid if I have complete faith, right?" His question had enough power to divert my attention from fear to curiosity.

I started thinking. *Did I pray during the take-off?* I think, yes. I was praying, but I think I was doing it out of fear, not faith. He was right. If I am afraid, it also means I don't have complete faith. "I agree with what you are saying, but I couldn't do anything else at that time other than just panic. Fear was very natural. It just occurred to me and I literally had no control over it. I think, all my efforts at that time were aimed at just getting me out of that phase. Do you have any better idea, by the way?"

The old man smiled again, with his face brightened this time. "Look at the other side of it. For the aircraft, take-off is a crucial step. It takes more efforts during this stage compared to the other stages of flight operation. But, in order to rise up against gravity, you require that kind of force, don't you? This happens in our life as well. To achieve the heights of success, you need to initially put in a lot of efforts against all the odds. Whatever it takes, you need to go through that initial phase. But at times, we feel that it is so hard and frightening that we just try to get out of it, instead of continuing with our efforts and faith."

I asked curiously, "Do you mean our life is all about the friction and struggle to achieve success?" The bright old man was excited to answer, "No. What I am saying here is that we can very well relate our life with the stages of the flight movement. The take-off phase is like a struggle before achieving success. The stable flight is like our journey after achieving the milestone. We still need to keep all the controls with us to maintain the course and direction of flight to ensure a safe journey. Landing is to relax, rejuvenate and refuel."

I was now really curious, "Oh! That's the great way to look at it. I never thought about it like this. I just kept thinking about how scary it would be. If you don't mind, may I request you to explain more about this? Because I think it will not only make my flight experience better, but also change the way I approach life."

The wise man explained "Sure! Why not? I would be delighted to share this with you. And I would be the happiest person on earth if this helps you. Let me explain it to you one by one:

1. **Take-off:** Most of the efforts are required in this phase, as there is maximum resistance from circumstances. Your ability, your experience, your knowledge, your precision and your courage, are all at test here. You have to perform under tremendous pressure. It is not impossible, but it is not easy either.

   You cannot do this unless you are prepared. You just cannot fake it. You may feel like quitting halfway, but there is no such choice. The same thing happens in life. Our most important turning points in life are often the most challenging and scary. They come at the most difficult times and life forces us to perform it under tremendous pressure. It leaves us with no other choice than just going through it.

   All forces against you, all the weight on your shoulders, all responsibility on your head and still you have no other choice than to perform.

   What do you do in such a situation? Do you give up? Or do you gather all your courage and just do it right? All great rewards in life come with efforts. The take-off stage teaches us the same thing. More the resistance and difficulty in achieving the task, the greater should be our preparation, more should be our efforts against it, overcoming all odds, focusing on our objective with relentless consistency and steadfast dedication. But we sometimes feel demotivated that circumstances are against us, people are not in our favour, nobody is there to support us and the task is too challenging for us. We give up, instead of identifying possibilities which might be already there for us to explore. And we miss the take-off. If it is required to go beyond the boundaries, then break all your limiting thoughts and make it possible.

In life, the most important aspect of the take-off phase for all of us to keep in mind, is that the success of the take-off phase completely depends on our preparation. Our preparation on professional skills and knowledge, preparation on health and energy, preparation on mindset and confidence, and preparation on our rituals and habits are important for the successful take-off of our professional and personal milestones in life.

2. **The flight:** The flight phase is all about maintaining your course, your altitude, attitude and speed. It's not just about achieving the desired altitude and direction. This is the phase where your alertness, consistency and discipline will be tested. Most importantly, we tend to get into the comfort zone after achieving the desired success initially. In the flight phase, we are at the higher altitude which also means higher risk level. We are susceptible to weather changes, air pockets and outside pressure changes. We also need to be attentive for communications with control towers

for any changes in navigation. It is also important to understand the technical challenges and make the necessary decisions to maintain smooth operations. At this stage, we should not forget that we have the responsibility of all the people who have boarded on the flight with complete faith in our knowledge and ability to operate the flight.

A similar thing happens in our life. When we achieve a certain level of success, we tend to get relaxed. We tend to lose the discipline, the fire in the belly which was there within us so far, our passion for progress and that driving force which kept us going throughout the challenging journey. I remember my first day in the gym. I was so excited and happy that I could finally manage to make this happen, despite my busy schedule. I was so excited to start taking care of my health and get disciplined. I was looking forward to great fitness and improved performance at my work. A few months later there was a significant improvement. It was actually better than what I'd initially expected. My performance at work improved so much that it actually helped me get promoted faster. But something happened after that and I slowly changed my rituals. I thought a new position is going to increase my stress levels and make me work more. So, I decided to take it easy and enjoy the life which I strongly felt I deserved. So, I changed my gym timing from early morning to after-office hours so I can get more sleep and wake up late every morning, which I felt was a very relaxing schedule. No rush, and yes, I deserve it at this stage of life, why take it so seriously, life is short and I need time for myself. For the next 6 months, I enjoyed my life, I ate the food which made me happy, I slept more than usual, I got the best gadgets to help me be more productive, I reduced all unnecessary activities which I thought may add to the stress. I was getting into a new territory of the 'comfort zone'. Everything was perfect till one fine day, after office hours, I started feeling uneasy. Suddenly, I started feeling that I needed to put in an effort to breath. It was not normal. I called my doctor friend.

After answering his questions, he asked me to see him at his clinic immediately. To my surprise, my blood pressure was high. Also, I realised that for the first time in the last six months, I was already overweight. The gym was not helpful, as I never attended it regularly. It was only in my mind that I had joined the gym, and that thought made me feel good all the time. Within 6 months, I lost my fitness due to this 'enjoy life' and 'I deserve it' mentality. In fact, it took me to an unhealthy lifestyle. My doctor friend asked me to continue taking medicines for the next 3 months, increase physical activities and manage my diet.

I was ignorant during my 'flight' phase. I was not serious enough to follow my rituals. I was not monitoring myself. I was away from my objectives. I would say I was away from myself. This had a huge impact on my performance at work. We missed the quarterly target. I was now serious. I started getting angry at myself. I finally told myself, enough is enough, I need to go back to the rituals which helped me for so many years and even during the most challenging situations. Things changed for the better in the next few months and I got back to my routine within a few months of struggle.

So, my dear friend, that was about the flight phase. Let's now go ahead with the next phase. I am sure you have a lot of questions running in your mind at this moment. But hold on for now. Let me first tell you about the landing phase.

3. **Landing:** This phase indicates the leisure break in your success journey. This is where you need to refuel and get recharged and make yourself prepared for the next take off. When we are at the peak of our success journey, we feel restless, we go on doing task after task. We become workaholics and are obsessed with success. We also feel that if we stop, we may lose our pace and it may impact our performance negatively. But as the flight needs to land after a certain interval and get refuelled and tested for technical issues, we also need to pause periodically and be with our selves. Now, we need to be careful here. A lot of break time can push you out of track. The break time used in a wrong way can also get you into negativity. The break should be chosen in such a way that it helps you to get recharged. Travelling to a new place, reading a great book, spending dedicated time with family, visiting an art gallery, spending time on your hobby or even going jogging or on a long walk. You can identify many great ways to use your break time to help you get refuelled."

I was carefully listening to this old man. Although I had so many questions in mind, I kept quiet and preferred to listen to his interesting philosophy, life's great lessons. This man first took me out of fear, then made me think about some of my decisions in life, shared the great philosophy of life from the simple example of flight. You must be very fortunate to meet such a co-passenger.

"Thank you so much. Your philosophy is so amazing. I now feel relaxed. I think this theory can be used to solve many situations in our life. I was just wondering if we can use this theory when we get stuck at a challenge?" I asked. He seemed to be expecting this question. He smiled and replied, "Yes, of course. You can use this theory at work and in life. Take any situation and apply this. Use the take-off principle to get to the action with push forward and break the procrastination. Let's take a few examples where you can apply this theory.

Flight Theory for Project Management: Use this at work when you are managing a project and you need to plan it. Make sure you are prepared with all the necessary background and requirements for the project, right from the resources, timelines, information required, financial support required, predictions about potential obstacles and plan to tackle it. You need to prepare in such a way as if you are preparing for take-off as a pilot of an aircraft. Once you are prepared, do not procrastinate, just go for the most difficult parts of the project and get it done by applying all your energy, creativity and knowledge. Once you complete the most challenging part, you can get back to the normal stage for the flight phase. As I told you, this phase is not for relaxing. Just make sure you are alert and watching all the controls, so that the the project is on the right altitude, speed and direction. After achieving the major milestones, just take a short break with your team and get refreshed before you embark on the next milestone.

Flight Theory for Personal Development: The flight theory is very useful in this area. Sometimes, you get distracted and lose the motivation to act. This theory helps you to get back to the preparation and ready yourself for take-off to the next learning stage. As you learn, you grow professionally. Consider every new skill you learn as a journey which involves all three phases of flight theory. Prepare, take-off, land and again prepare for the next take-off of a new skillset.

Flight Theory for Doing Hard Things in life: The challenging things in life are like the take-off stage. Understand the requirements, prepare every possible thing about it, gather the courage and energy required to lift it against gravity and then apply that power and take-off. Break the barriers and make things happen using the flight theory.

Flight Theory when you are afraid: Just think about flight theory. It tells you that big things in life are achieved by going beyond fear. If you are afraid, nothing is going to happen. No one is going to help you. Instead just prepare for the take-off into new territory. Put the maximum possible efforts and use all your power to make it happen. Prepare, instead of being afraid, because every success will bring uncertainty with it. Nothing is certain in this world. So, don't waste your time in being afraid. A successful take-off takes you to higher altitudes which are risky for flight operations. While you come back to the ground, the landing is not easy. It takes great skill to land safely. So, instead of just being afraid about it, go for it."

I was so impressed to listen to this man, "That's really wonderful. I think I can now apply this theory in the various areas of my life. Sometimes, I get demotivated by looking at the massive challenge of the task and I procrastinate over it. I think this theory is going to be very useful in such situations. Thanks a lot. You have given me such a great gift of life today. I do not have more words to thank you."

The old man said, "I am happy that it was helpful to you. I am sure you will share this philosophy with others and help them get fearless and motivated and happily solve the challenges of life." We smiled at each other and continued exchanging our thoughts during the further part of the journey. It was the most memorable journey for me. I decided to use this theory and also share it with others.

THE HUMAN ECLIPSE

All love is expansion, all selfishness is contraction. Love is therefore the only law of life. He who loves lives, he who is selfish is dying. Therefore, love for love's sake, because it is the only law of life, just as you breathe to live.

– Swami Vivekananda

This is the age of violence. As soon as our television is switched on, we get to know about the bombing, killing, fighting, the wars and so many other insane things happening in some part of the world or other. It is much beyond just loss of lives and loss of property. It is about the loss of values, ethics and the sense of being human. One of the basic differences between humans and animals is their respective place in the food chain. Animals kill each other to survive, humans don't. In fact, humans don't need to do that. The sustainability of human lives comes from the principle of co-existence. We seek happiness from life, not just food and safety. Evolution helped us to get better at what we do and ensure our happiness. For the very fact that evolution is a natural process, we should not even worry about our future, for it is going to get better continuously. Every new generation will have more intelligence than the previous one. All we need to do is to keep up our good work as we have been doing for ages. We must not forget where and why it all started, the basic purpose of humanity, our responsibility towards the coming generations and towards this planet, our unlimited capabilities and intelligence, our ancestor's work and the path laid down by them. It is not just about survival, but about our culture, language, food, social protocols, philosophy of life, habits and rituals developed by various groups and communities, interaction with the environment, love and care, trust and loyalty and so many characteristics we possess as human beings. It is not developed overnight, it took years of efforts to reach to our lifestyle today.

But there are times when we do things which are not aligned with our purpose. Let's call it the 'Human Eclipse' where we come under the dark shadow of the unknown and lose our direction. This is the eclipse of our own thoughts, our own habits and our own beliefs which takes us to the unknown territory. Any unknown is frustrating for humans. We start behaving like animals and lose harmony. Once we are of the opinion that we need to fight for survival, the new journey begins with the animal inside us. Thoughtless actions follow. You kill everything that you believe is dangerous to your life, dangerous to your family, dangerous to your community and dangerous to your country. We do things as if we have the right to destroy everything around us, hoping to get out of the frustration, get out of the eclipse, just to fail. On the one hand, we talk about colonising Mars, and on the other hand we are killing the colonies we created on our existing planet. There is a big contradiction in our behaviour and our purpose. As humans, we are supposed to help each other get the real benefits of evolution regarding connectivity, mobility, accessibility, liveability and betterment of this planet. It is our responsibility to protect our values, our lives, our cultures so that the next generations carry the message with them.

Happiness lies in love and harmony among us. Let's get out of all these Human Eclipses which jeopardise us. They are the real threat to our existence.

Every one of us is a human being with heart and mind and hence it is very natural that we have feelings of love towards humanity and nature on this planet. We understand everyone's needs and we respect each other. We know the importance of common resources available on this planet, which is essential for living. But sometimes, we start comparing ourselves with others and get into the eclipse of our insecurities and illusions. We carry uncertainties in our minds and blame each other for that. When we do not get answers, we get into the defensive mode. We feel threatened by each other and attack others to safeguard ourselves. The violence begins and everything gets destroyed in it – lives, resources, relations, feelings, love and humanity. The darkness of human eclipse is so evil that it makes us defeat ourselves in this process.

What a sad end to life if we waste our time in defeating ourselves and destroying this planet. What a shameful life if we forget the very purpose of this life and betray our own roots. What a foolishness if we fall for tricks of negativity and sell our principles and values that we have earned by years and years of the evolution process. What an irony if we call ourselves the most intelligent and wise species ever created by God and, at the same time, act so silly as if we have completely lost our wisdom. What a failure of life if we do not contribute towards the betterment of humanity and protection of our own planet. What a huge disappointment for God who gifted us amazing creative powers and sent us to this planet, and we are using those powers just to destroy all his creations.

Let's stop these senseless acts. Let's understand our responsibilities and duties to continue and contribute to the evolution process. Let's come together and work for the sustainability of the earth for the sake of future generations. Let's protect our limited resources and our earned values to make this place better day by day. Let's start helping each other for our responsibility towards humanity. Let's safeguard ourselves from the shadow of the human eclipse.

THE MESSAGE FROM GOD

Oh, my dear child,

I am sending you to the beautiful world of planet earth, I have created with so much love, and it is your job to protect it, help it, save it and nurture it.

I have decided a special role for you to perform there, and hence certain things are predefined for you.

I am giving you plenty of choices, with a challenge of choosing the best for you.

To make it an adventure for you, I will not tell you the specific purpose of your life, as you have to find it out yourself.

For this reason, I will give you hints and indications time to time, make sure you are alert to listen to it and mindful enough to interpret it right.

To make your stay interesting, I will give you different phases in your life from childhood to teenage to young age to old age.

As a part of your duty, I hope you will help planet earth to get better, I will see you again here to talk about your achievements.

For your joy, I will give you vivid seasons, situations and various kinds of people around you; I am also gifting you with the secret power of love so that you can connect with people.

I hope you spend your time wisely and happily. I have provided you with all the abilities I can think of. Your job is to make use of them and help my planet to get better in every possible way.

It is your responsibility to use your mind and body in such a way that you achieve the objective and come back to me with happiness and accomplishment.

Keep in mind, in the end I will not count what you collect, but I will count what you create in the process of improving my planet.

I wish you a very exciting journey through life!

With Love!

www.ingramcontent.com/pod-product-compliance
Lightning Source LLC
La Vergne TN
LVHW042343150826
845671LV00001B/7

* 9 7 9 8 8 9 5 1 9 0 6 0 9 *